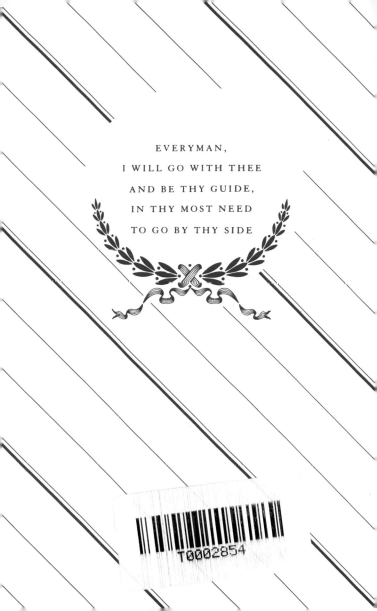

EVERYMAN,
I WILL GO WITH THEE
AND BE THY GUIDE,
IN THY MOST NEED
TO GO BY THY SIDE

T0002854

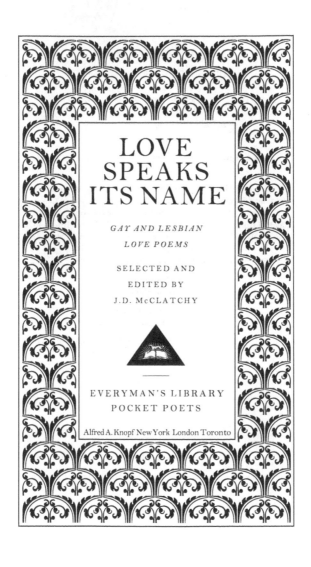

LOVE SPEAKS ITS NAME

GAY AND LESBIAN
LOVE POEMS

SELECTED AND
EDITED BY
J.D. McCLATCHY

EVERYMAN'S LIBRARY
POCKET POETS

Alfred A. Knopf New York London Toronto

THIS IS A BORZOI BOOK

PUBLISHED BY ALFRED A. KNOPF

This selection by J. D. McClatchy first published in
Everyman's Library, 2001
Copyright © 2001 by Everyman's Library

Seventh printing (US)

www.randomhouse.com/everymans
www.everymanslibrary.co.uk

ISBN 978-0-375-41170-0 (US)
978-1-84159-745-4 (UK)

A CIP catalogue record for this book is available from the British Library

Typography by Peter B. Willberg

Typeset in the UK by AccComputing, North Barrow, Somerset

Printed and bound in Germany by GGP Media GmbH, Pössneck

CONTENTS

8

FOREWORD

This is a book, first of all, about desire. A desire can be a vague wish, a sharp craving, a steadfast longing, a helpless obsession. It can signal an absence or a presence, a need or a commitment, an ideal or an impossibility. The root of the word "desire" links it to *consider* and to terms for investigation and augury, thereby reminding us that desire is often less what we feel than what we think about what we feel. And the still deeper root of the word links it to *star* and *shine*, as if our desires, the bright centers of our being, were also like the fixed fates in the heavens, determining the course of our lives. Indeed, our mundane experience of desire often coincides with this sense of something beyond our control, of something confusing, something driving us beyond the bounds of habit or reason. It is the heart of our hearts, the very stuff of the self. Desire explodes past borders of time or law. It drifts through veils of propriety. It cannot be confined by social expectations or strictures.

Love is something else again. As mysterious as are the ways of desire, and as disconcerting its effects, love is desire raised to a higher power. It can he as consuming as desire, but it lasts longer. Love is the quality of attention we pay to things. Love is both the shrine and the idol. Love is what we make of other people, and what they make of us. It can be as dispassionate as a Zen monk's, or as wasting as the Romantic hero's. Love affairs can be sentimental melodramas, bittersweet comedies, or five-act tragedies, but they are always dramatic, building from first glance to last goodbye. Love has nothing to do with behavior or circumstances. Love doesn't require sexual expression, or even a meeting, just as it continues, often stronger, after the beloved's death.

So, this is a book, in the end, about both desire and its higher power, about love in its tender or taunting variety. And the poems here have all been written by men and women whose desires for love, over the centuries, have been condemned and persecuted. In earlier days this forced them to learn how to disguise their desires. But then, that is what poems do as well. To hide something is to conceal it; to disguise something is to reveal it but only to those who know how and where to look. The very conventions of poetry were devised to encode experience, to make it less obvious and thereby more true. To make a metaphor, after all, is to describe something in terms of what it is *not*, the better to apprehend what it *is*. In ages when to reveal one's homosexuality risked imprisonment or death, the poet had better be oblique. A lesbian poet might address her beloved in the voice of a man. A gay poet might pretend to rhapsodize over a mythological boy or abstract figure. That anyone would be proscribed from celebrating love seems, from today's more enlightened but still fraught vantage, altogether shameful. Between classical times and the Renaissance, the poetry of homosexuality was largely underground, as indeed it remained for four more centuries, until a distinctive homosexual culture emerged in the late nineteenth century. With such a history of persecution to contend with, it is no wonder that poets who happened to be homosexual turned their sense of exclusion into a source of poetic strength. Over the centuries, the homosexual temperament has seemed especially suited to engaging the themes of bafflement, secret joys, private perspectives, forbidden paradises, hypocritical conventions, and ecstatic occasions. In fact, it would be fair to claim that our gay and lesbian poets are the wisest inquirers after love. Love, after all, takes the strangest forms. For the last two thousand years, for instance, the most vicious persecutors of homosexuals have all been huddled under a banner that reads "Love Thy Neighbor." Our lesbian and gay poets have been forced to learn love's harshest lessons the better to understand its sweetest instructions. They know more about what is disallowed in the pursuit of happiness, more about the false leads and wrong turns of passion, more about the emergencies of a double life, more about love's secret passages, its private mythologies, its defiant pride, its beguiling joy.

15

If love can be any life's true contentment, it is also a restless emotion. That is why this book circles love's stages. As it happens, the shortest section of poems here deals with love's blissful extremes. "Love," wrote Chekhov, perhaps a little too glumly, "is either the shrinking remnant of something which was once enormous; or else it is part of something which will grow in the future into something enormous. But in the present it does not satisfy. It gives much less than one expects." Or more. In any case, it can begin with an ache in the heart, an emptiness only discovered by what will fill it. Or a slight fancy unexpectedly takes a complicated shape. As Mark Doty's poem puts it, longing "becomes its own object, the way/that desire can make anything into a god." So longing yields to looking, the lover's rapt gaze, the eye both eager and shy. The poems in praise of love in this anthology have been written by many of the masters of the art, from Walt Whitman, Hart Crane, and Gertrude Stein to Elizabeth Bishop, May Swenson, and W. H. Auden. And there are poets from around the world or from ancient times — Sappho or Michelangelo. Cavafy or García Lorca. Each brings an unusual lens to bear on a complicated subject. All these poems can be witty or heartbreaking, by turns or at once. Each is a mood, a moment, a meditation of what is abiding and evanescent.

Anxiety is sewn into the lining of euphoria. What makes the beloved so dear, what makes love so precious, is the realization that it may – no, in the end, it *will* – end. Always, as Djuna Barnes notes, "hidden underground the soft moles drowse." Love's illusions are constructed in order to be undermined. Vulnerability, not music, is the food of love. Our fears are the black backing of our silvered hopes, and are as much a part of love as are the anticipation and the fervor. And when love evaporates or ends? Perhaps the most poignant stage of love is not its tender antennae probing the new surface, and not the glistening track of its progress. but the shell into which it retreats for shelter. Neither betrayal nor death can end our love. The force of memory, and the heart's persistent needs see to that. "When I am dead," writes Muriel Rukeyser, "even then/I am still listening to you." Poems are meant to embody and eternalize the moment. So too are our memories of a love, just as love itself, when we are in the grip of it, throws off the shackles of time and makes us – for a moment that seems forever – feel divine.

All the poets in this book, like their sisters and brothers in ages past, were dealt an unusual hand. I don't mean just the fact that they were born with a particular set of desires. They were born with a particular set of ambitions – to be poets: to take the flesh and make it a word. Their poems about love are among the most perceptive and exultant we have. Because their desires have been deemed dangerous, and their lives made difficult, they place a unique value on true love. There are no simple formulas in this book. Pleasure has been wrung from pain, illumination wrested from bitterness and fear, the moment of transcendence stolen from complacent hours. The results may startle or thrill. But here is the very life of love in all its complexity. Here is the art of poetry – daring, darting, connecting, consoling – at its best.

J. D. MCCLATCHY

LONGING

"BE KIND TO ME"

Be kind to me

Gongyla; I ask only
that you wear the cream
white dress when you come

Desire darts about your
loveliness, drawn down in
circling flight at sight of it

and I am glad, although
once I too quarrelled
with Aphrodite
           to whom
I pray that you will
come soon

PRAYER TO MY LADY
OF PAPHOS

Dapple-throned Aphrodite,
eternal daughter of God,
snare-knitter! Don't, I beg you,

cow my heart with grief! Come,
as once when you heard my far-
off cry and, listening, stepped

from your father's house to your
gold car, to yoke the pair whose
beautiful thick-feathered wings

oaring down mid-air from heaven
carried you to light swiftly
on dark earth; then, blissful one,

smiling your immortal smile
you asked, What ailed me now that
made me call you again? What

was it that my distracted
heart most wanted? "Whom has
Persuasion to bring round now

"to your love? Who, Sappho, is
unfair to you? For, let her
run, she will soon run after;

"if she won't accept gifts, she
will one day give them; and if
she won't love you – she soon will

"love, although unwillingly. . . ."
If ever – come now! Relieve
this intolerable pain!

What my heart most hopes will
happen, make happen; you your-
self join forces on my side!

SONNET 29

When in disgrace with Fortune and men's eyes,
I all alone beweep my outcast state,
And trouble deaf heaven with my bootless cries,
And look upon myself and curse my fate,
Wishing me like to one more rich in hope,
Featured like him, like him with friends possessed,
Desiring this man's art and that man's scope,
With what I most enjoy contented least –
Yet in these thoughts myself almost despising,
Haply I think on thee, and then my state,
Like to the lark at break of day arising
From sullen earth, sings hymns at heaven's gate.
  For thy sweet love remembered such wealth brings
  That then I scorn to change my state with kings.

From EDWARD II (Act I, Scene I)

GAVESTON (reading a letter from Edward):

"My father is deceas'd. Come, Gaveston,
And share the kingdom with thy dearest friend."
Ah, words that make me surfeit with delight!
What greater bliss can hap to Gaveston
Than live and be the favourite of a king!
Sweet prince, I come! These, these thy amorous lines
Might have enforc'd me to have swum from France,
And, like Leander, gasp'd upon the sand,
So thou wouldst smile, and take me in thine arms.
The sight of London to my exil'd eyes
Is as Elysium to a new-come soul:
Not that I love the city or the men,
But that it harbours him I hold so dear –
The king, upon whose bosom let me die,
And with the world be still at enmity.

CHRISTOPHER MARLOWE   25

SONNET

Here, hold this glove (this milk-white cheveril glove)
   Not quaintly over-wrought with curious knots,
   Not deckt with golden spangs, nor silver spots,
Yet wholesome for thy hand as thou shalt prove.
Ah no; (sweet boy) place this glove neere thy heart,
   Weare it, and lodge it still within thy brest,
   So shalt thou make me (most unhappy), blest.
So shalt thou rid my paine, and ease my smart:
How can that be (perhaps) thou wilt reply,
   A glove is for the hand not for the heart,
   Nor can it well be prov'd by common art,
Nor reasons rule. To this, thus answere I:
   If thou from glove do'st take away the g,
   Then glove is love: and so I send it thee.

SECOND ECLOGUE

Young *Corydon*, th' unhappy Shepherd Swain,
The fair *Alexis* lov'd, but lov'd in vain:
And underneath the Beechen Shade, alone,
Thus to the Woods and Mountains made his moan.
Is this, unkind *Alexis*, my reward,
And must I die unpitied, and unheard?
Now the green Lizard in the Grove is laid,
The Sheep enjoy the coolness of the Shade;
And *Thestilis* wild Thime and Garlike beats
For Harvest Hinds, o'erspent with Toyl and Heats:
While in the scorching Sun I trace in vain
Thy flying footsteps o'er the burning Plain.
The creaking Locusts with my Voice conspire,
They fry'd with Heat, and I with fierce Desire.
How much more easie was it to sustain
Proud *Amarillis*, and her haughty Reign,
The Scorns of Young *Menalcas*, once my care,
Tho' he was black, and thou art Heav'nly fair.
Trust not too much to that enchanting Face;
Beauty's a Charm, but soon the Charm will pass:
White Lillies lie neglected on the Plain,
While dusky Hyacinths for use remain.
My Passion is thy Scorn; nor wilt thou know
What Wealth I have, what Gifts I can bestow:
What Stores my Dairies and my Folds contain;

A thousand Lambs that wander on the Plain:
New Milk that all the Winter never fails,
And all the Summer overflows the Pails:
Amphion sung not sweeter to his Herd,
When summon'd Stones the *Theban* Turrets rear'd.
Nor am I so deform'd; for late I stood
Upon the Margin of the briny Flood:
The Winds were still, and if the Glass be true,
With *Daphnis* I may vie, tho' judg'd by you.
O leave the noisie Town, O come and see
Our Country Cotts, and live content with me!
To wound the Flying Deer, and from their Cotes
With me to drive a-Field, the browzing Goats:
To pipe and sing, and in our Country Strain
To Copy, or perhaps contend with *Pan.*
Pan taught to joyn with Wax unequal Reeds,
Pan loves the Shepherds, and their Flocks he feeds:
Nor scorn the Pipe; *Amyntas,* to be taught,
With all his Kisses would my Skill have bought.
Of seven smooth joints a mellow Pipe I have,
Which with his dying Breath *Damaetas* gave:
And said, This, *Corydon,* I leave to thee;
For only thou deserv'st it after me.
His Eyes *Amyntas* durst not upward lift,
For much he grudg'd the Praise, but more the Gift.
Besides two Kids that in the Valley stray'd,

I found by chance and to my fold convey'd.
They drein two bagging Udders every day;
And these shall be Companions of thy Play.
Both fleck'd with white, the true *Arcadian* Strain,
Which *Thestilis* had often beg'd in vain:
And she shall have them, if again she sues,
Since you the Giver and the Gift refuse.
Come to my longing Arms, my lovely care,
And take the Presents which the Nymphs prepare.
White Lillies in full Canisters they bring,
With all the Glories of the Purple Spring:
The Daughters of the Flood have search'd the Mead
For Violets pale, and cropt the Poppy's Head:
The Short *Narcissus* and fair Daffodil,
Pancies to please the Sight, and Cassia sweet to smell:
And set soft Hyacinths with Iron blue,
To shade marsh Marigolds of shining Hue.
Some bound in Order, others loosely strow'd,
To dress thy Bow'r, and trim thy new Abode.
My self will search our planted Grounds at home,
For downy Peaches and the glossie Plum:
And thrash the Chesnuts in the Neighb'ring Grove,
Such as my *Amarillis* us'd to love.
The Laurel and the Myrtle sweets agree;
And both in Nosegays shall be bound for thee.
Ah, *Corydon*, ah poor unhappy Swain,

Alexis will thy homely Gifts disdain:
Nor, should'st thou offer all thy little Store,
Will rich *Iolas* yield, but offer more.
What have I done, to name that wealthy Swain,
So powerful are his Presents, mine so mean!
The Boar amidst my Crystal Streams I bring;
And Southern Winds to blast my flow'ry Spring.
Ah, cruel Creature, whom dost thou despise?
The Gods to live in Woods have left the Skies.
And Godlike *Paris* in th' *Idean* Grove,
To *Priam*'s Wealth prefer'd *Oenone*'s Love.
In Cities which she built, let *Pallas* Reign;
Tow'rs are for Gods, but Forrests for the Swain.
The greedy Lyoness the Wolf pursues,
The Wolf the Kid, the wanton Kid the Browze:
Alexis thou art chas'd by *Corydon*;
All follow sev'ral Games, and each his own.
See from afar the Fields no longer smoke,
The sweating Steers unharness'd from the Yoke,
Bring, as in Triumph, back the crooked Plough;
The Shadows lengthen as the Sun goes Low.
Cool Breezes now the raging Heats remove;
Ah, cruel Heaven! that made no Cure for Love!
I wish for balmy Sleep, but wish in vain:
Love has no bounds in Pleasure, or in Pain.
What frenzy, Shepherd, has thy Soul possess'd,

Thy Vinyard lies half prun'd, and half undress'd.
Quench, *Corydon*, thy long unanswer'd fire:
Mind what the common wants of Life require.
On willow Twigs employ thy weaving care:
And find an easier Love, tho' not so fair.

LOVE MISINTERPRETED

If the undying thirst that purifies
our mortal thoughts, could draw mine to the day,
perchance the lord who now holds cruel sway
in Love's high house, would prove more kindly-wise.

But since the laws of heaven immortalise
our souls, and doom our flesh to swift decay,
tongue cannot tell how fair, how pure as day,
is the soul's thirst that far beyond it lies.

How then, ah wo is me! shall that chaste fire,
which burns the heart within me, be made known,
if sense finds only sense in what it sees?

All my fair hours are turned to miseries
with my loved lord, who minds but lies alone;
for, truth to tell, who trusts not is a liar.

AT BAIA

I should have thought
in a dream you would have brought
some lovely, perilous thing,
orchids piled in a great sheath,
as who would say (in a dream)
I send you this,
who left the blue veins
of your throat unkissed.

Why was it that your hands
(that never took mine)
your hands that I could see
drift over the orchid heads
so carefully,
your hands, so fragile, sure to lift
so gently, the fragile flower stuff –
ah, ah, how was it

You never sent (in a dream)
the very form, the very scent,
not heavy, not sensuous,
but perilous – perilous –
of orchids, piled in a great sheath,
and folded underneath on a bright scroll
some word:

Flower sent to flower;
for white hands, the lesser white,
less lovely of flower leaf

or

Lover to lover, no kiss,
no touch, but forever and ever this.

NO OBLIGATION

Come on the wings of great desire,
    Or stay away from me.
You're not more stable than the day,
    Or than the day less free.

The dawning day has clouds in store;
    Desire her cloudy moods;
And sunlit woods of morning may
    By noon be darkened woods.

So be you free to come or stay
    Without a reason given,
As free as clouds that blot the light
    Across the face of heaven.

THE LETTER

Little cramped words scrawling all over the paper
Like draggled fly's legs,
What can you tell of the flaring moon
Through the oak leaves?
Or of my uncurtained window and the bare floor
Spattered with moonlight?
Your silly quirks and twists have nothing in them
Of blossoming hawthorns,
And this paper is dull, crisp, smooth, virgin of
    loveliness
Beneath my hand.

I am tired, Beloved, of chafing my heart against
The want of you;
Of squeezing it into little inkdrops,
And posting it.
And I scald alone, here, under the fire
Of the great moon.

THE POET SPEAKS WITH HIS BELOVED ON THE TELEPHONE

Your voice watered the dune of my breast
in the sweet wooden booth.
South of my feet, it was Spring,
and north of my brow, a fern blossomed.

Within that narrow space a pine of light
sang out, but with no dawn, no seed to sow;
and my lament for the first time
hung coronets of hope upon the roof.

Sweet and distant voice, spilling for me.
Sweet and distant voice, tasted by me.
Distant and sweet voice, muffled softly.

Distant like a dark and wounded doe.
Sweet like sobbing during the fall of snow.
Distant and sweet, and caught in the marrow!

FEDERICO GARCÍA LORCA   37
TRANSLATED BY JOHN K. WALSH AND
FRANCISCO ARAGON

SONNET OF THE GARLAND OF ROSES

That garland! Hurry please! For I am dying!
Weave quickly now! And sing! And moan! And sing!
For the shadow is darkening my throat
and January light returns a thousand times.

Between your love for me and mine for you
lies star-filled air and the trembling of a plant.
A thicket of anemones is lifting
with dark moaning, an entire year.

So relish the fresh landscape of my wound,
break open delicate rivulets and reeds,
and sip the blood spilled on the honeyed thigh.

But hurry, so together, intertwined,
mouths bruised with love and souls bitten,
time will find us wasted.

38   FEDERICO GARCÍA LORCA
     TRANSLATED BY JOHN K. WALSH AND
     FRANCISCO ARAGON

"WHAT'S IN YOUR MIND, MY DOVE"

What's in your mind, my dove, my coney;
Do thoughts grow like feathers, the dead end of life;
Is it making of love or counting of money,
Or raid on the jewels, the plans of a thief?

Open your eyes, my dearest dallier;
Let hunt with your hands for escaping me;
Go through the motions of exploring the familiar;
Stand on the brink of the warm white day.

Rise with the wind, my great big serpent;
Silence the birds and darken the air;
Change me with terror, alive in a moment;
Strike for the heart and have me there.

HE ASKED ABOUT THE QUALITY

He left the office where he'd taken up
a trivial, poorly paid job
(eight pounds a month, including bonuses) –
left at the end of the dreary work
that kept him bent all afternoon,
came out at seven and walked off slowly,
idling his way down the street. Good-looking;
and interesting: showing as he did that he'd reached
his full sensual capacity.
He'd turned twenty-nine the month before.

He idled his way down the main street
and the poor side-streets that led to his home.

Passing in front of a small shop
that sold cheap and flimsy things for workers.
he saw a face inside there, saw a figure
that compelled him to go in, and he pretended
he wanted to look at some colored handkerchiefs.

He asked about the quality of the handkerchiefs
and how much they cost, his voice choking,
almost silenced by desire.
And the answers came back the same way,
distracted, the voice hushed,
offering hidden consent.

They kept on talking about the merchandise – but
the only purpose: that their hands might touch
over the handkerchiefs, that their faces, their lips,
might move close together as though by chance –
a moment's meeting of limb against limb.

Quickly, secretly, so the shopowner sitting at
        the back
wouldn't realize what was going on.

CONSTANTINE CAVAFY
TRANSLATED BY EDMUND KEELEY
AND PHILIP SHERRARD

MUNICH, WINTER 1973
(for Y. S.)

In a strange house,
a strange bed
in a strange town,
a very strange me
is waiting for you.

Now
it is very early in the morning.
The silence is loud.
The baby is walking about
with his foaming bottle,
making strange sounds
and deciding, after all,
to be my friend.

You
arrive tonight.

How dull time is!
How empty – and yet,
since I am sitting here,
lying here,
walking up and down here,
waiting,

I see
that time's cruel ability
to make one wait
is time's reality.

I see your hair
which I call red.
I lie here in this bed.

Someone teased me once,
a friend of ours –
saying that I saw your hair red
because I was not thinking
of the hair on your head.

Someone also told me,
a long time ago:
my father said to me,
It is a terrible thing,
son,
to fall into the hands of the living God.
Now,
I know what he was saying.
I could not have seen red

before finding myself
in this strange, this waiting bed.
Nor had my naked eye suggested
that colour was created
by the light falling, now,
on me,
in this strange bed,
waiting
where no one has ever rested!

The streets, I observe,
are wintry.
It feels like snow.
Starlings circle in the sky,
conspiring,
together, and alone,
unspeakable journeys
into and out of the light.

I know
I will see you tonight.
And snow
may fall
enough to freeze our tongues
and scald our eyes.
We may never be found again!

Just as the birds above our heads
circling
are singing,
knowing
that, in what lies before them,
the always unknown passage,
wind, water, air,
the failing light
the falling night
the blinding sun
they must get the journey done.
Listen.
They have wings and voices
are making choices
are using what they have.
They are aware
that, on long journeys,
each bears the other,
whirring,
stirring
love occurring
in the middle of the terrifying air.

SUNDAY

The mint bed is in
bloom: lavender haze
day. The grass is
more than green and
throws up sharp and
cutting lights to
slice through the
plane tree leaves. And
on the cloudless blue
I scribble your name.

From LAST POEMS

XXVI

The half-moon westers low, my love,
  And the wind brings up the rain;
And wide apart lie we, my love,
  And seas between the twain.

I know not if it rains, my love,
  In the land where you do lie;
And oh, so sound you sleep, my love,
  You know no more than I.

From A SHROPSHIRE LAD

XI

On your midnight pallet lying,
    Listen, and undo the door:
Lads that waste the light in sighing
    In the dark should sigh no more;
Night should ease a lover's sorrow;
Therefore, since I go to-morrow,
    Pity me before.

In the land to which I travel,
    The far dwelling, let me say —
Once, if here the couch is gravel,
    In a kinder bed I lay,
And the breast the darnel smothers
Rested once upon another's
    When it was not clay.

MAD ABOUT THE BOY

Mad about the boy,
It's pretty funny but I'm mad about the boy,
He has a gay appeal
That makes me feel
There's maybe something sad about the boy.
Walking down the street,
His eyes look out at me from people that I meet,
I can't believe it's true
But when I'm blue
In some strange way I'm glad about the boy.
I'm hardly sentimental,
Love isn't so sublime,
I have to pay my rental
And I can't afford to waste much time,
If I could employ
A little magic that would finally destroy
This dream that pains me
And enchains me,
But I can't because I'm mad about the boy.

POEM

I will always love you
though I never loved you

a boy smelling faintly of heather
staring up at your window

the passion that enlightens
and stills and cultivates, gone

while I sought your face
to be familiar in the blueness

or to follow your sharp whistle
around a corner into my light

that was love growing fainter
each time you failed to appear

I spent my whole self searching
love which I thought was you

it was mine so briefly
and I never knew it, or you went

I thought it was outside disappearing
but it is disappearing in my heart

like snow blown in a window
to be gone from the world

I will always love you

THE KIMONO

When I returned from lovers' lane
My hair was white as snow.
Joy, incomprehension, pain
I'd seen like seasons come and go.
How I got home again
Frozen half dead, perhaps you know.

You hide a smile and quote a text:
Desires ungratified
Persist from one life to the next.
Hearths we strip ourselves beside
Long, long ago were x'd
On blueprints of "consuming pride."

Times out of mind, the bubble-gleam
To our charred level drew
April back. A sudden beam . . .
— Keep talking while I change into
The pattern of a stream
Bordered with rushes white on blue.

SYMMETRICAL COMPANION

It must be
there walks somewhere in the world
another
another namely like me

Not twin
but opposite
as my two hands are opposite

Where are you
my symmetrical companion?

Do you inhabit
the featureless fog
of the future?
Are you sprinting
from the shadows of the past
to overtake me?
Or are you camouflaged
in the colored present?
Do I graze you every day
as yet immune to your touch
unaware of your scent
inert under your glance?

Come to me
Whisper your name
I will know you instantly
by a passport
decipherable to ourselves alone

We shall walk uniformed
in our secret
We shall be a single reversible cloak
lined with light within
furred with dark without

Nothing shall be forbidden us
All bars shall fall before us
Even the past shall be lit behind us
and seen to have led
like two predestined corridors
to the vestibule of our meeting

We shall be two daring acrobats
above the staring faces
framed in wheels of light
visible to millions
yet revealed only to each other
in the tiny circular mirrors
of our pupils

We shall climb together
up the frail ladders
balancing on slender
but steel-strong thongs of faith
When you leap
my hands will be surely there
at the arc's limit
We shall synchronize
each step of the dance upon the wire
We shall not fall
as long as our gaze is not severed

Where are you
my symmetrical companion?

Until I find you
my mouth is locked
my heart is numb
my mind unlit
my limbs unjointed

I am a marionette
doubled up in a dark trunk
a dancer frozen
in catatonic sleep
a statue locked
in the stone

a Lazarus wrapped
in the swaddling strips
not of death
but of unborn life

a melody bound
in the strings of the viol
a torrent imprisoned
in ice
a flame buried
in the coal
a jewel hidden
in a block of lava

Come release me
Without you I do not yet exist

THE DEATH OF ANTINOÜS

When the beautiful young man drowned –
accidentally, swimming at dawn
in a current too swift for him,
or obedient to some cult
of total immersion that promised
the bather would come up divine,

mortality rinsed from him –
Hadrian placed his image everywhere,
a marble Antinoüs staring across
the public squares where a few dogs
always scuffled, planted
in every squalid little crossroad

at the farthest corners of the Empire.
What do we want in any body
but the world? And if the lover's
inimitable form was nowhere,
then he would find it everywhere,
though the boy became simply more dead

as the sculptors embodied him.
Wherever Hadrian might travel,
the beloved figure would be there
first: the turn of his shoulders,

the exact marble nipples,
the drowned face not really lost

to the Nile – which has no appetite,
merely takes in anything
without judgment or expectation –
but lost into its own multiplication,
an artifice rubbed with oils and acid
so that the skin might shine.

Which of these did I love?
Here is his hair, here his hair
again. Here the chiseled liquid waist
I hold because I cannot hold it.
If only one of you, he might have said
to any of the thousand marble boys anywhere,

would speak. Or the statues might have been enough,
the drowned boy blurred as much by memory
as by water, molded toward an essential,
remote ideal. Longing, of course,
becomes its own object, the way
that desire can make anything into a god.

BEWITCHED, BOTHERED
AND BEWILDERED

I'm wild again,
Beguiled again,
A simpering, whimpering child again –
Bewitched, bothered and bewildered am I.
Couldn't sleep
And wouldn't sleep
Until I could sleep where I shouldn't sleep –
Bewitched, bothered and bewildered am I.
Lost my heart, but what of it?
My mistake, I agree.
He's a laugh, but I love it
Because the laugh's on me.
A pill he is,
But still he is
All mine and I'll keep him until he is
Bewitched, bothered and bewildered
Like me.

Seen a lot –
I mean a lot –
But now I'm like sweet seventeen a lot –
Bewitched, bothered and bewildered am I.
I'll sing to him,
Each spring to him,

And worship the trousers that cling to him –
Bewitched, bothered and bewildered am I.
When he talks, he is seeking
Words to get off his chest.
Horizontally speaking,
He's at his very best.
Vexed again,
Perplexed again,
Thank God I can be oversexed again –
Bewitched, bothered and bewildered am I.

SEPTEMBER

This isn't being in love for a very first time.
Nor is it some new flu leaving me weak, feverish.
It's missing you. All the nectar sucked
Right out of my heart, your look, your talk, your habits.

An autumnal restlessness: picking my way down
The hill through bracken, knee-deep and turning
Russet underneath; and where it thins out, occasional
Clumps of harebells. Their delicate blue, desire's.

LOOKING

SONNET

Sporting at fancie, setting light by love,
　　There came a theefe, and stole away my heart,
　　(And therefore rob'd me of my chiefest part)
Yet cannot Reason him a felon prove.
For why his beauty (my hearts thiefe) affirmeth,
　　Piercing no skin (the bodies fensive wall)
　　And having leave, and free consent withall,
Himselfe not guilty, from love guilty tearmeth,
Conscience the Judge, twelve Reasons are the Jurie,
　　They finde mine eies the beutie t' have let in,
　　And on this verdict given, agreed they bin,
Wherefore, because his beauty did allure yee,
　　Your Doome is this; in teares still to be drowned,
　　When his faire forehead with disdain is frowned.

RICHARD BARNFIELD

A GLIMPSE

A glimpse through an interstice caught,
Of a crowd of workmen and drivers in a bar-room
      around the stove late of a winter night, and I
      unremark'd seated in a corner,
Of a youth who loves me and whom I love, silently
      approaching and seating himself near, that he may
      hold me by the hand,
A long while amid the noises of coming and going, of
      drinking and oath and smutty jest,
There we two, content, happy in being together,
      speaking little, perhaps not a word.

AMONG THE MULTITUDE

Among the men and women the multitude,
I perceive one picking me out by secret and
    divine signs,
Acknowledging none else, not parent, wife, husband,
    brother, child, any nearer than I am,
Some are baffled, but that one is not – that one
    knows me.

Ah lover and perfect equal,
I meant that you should discover me so by faint
    indirections,
And I when I meet you mean to discover you
    by the like in you.

AT A DINNER PARTY

With fruit and flowers the board is decked,
    The wine and laughter flow;
I'll not complain – could one expect
    So dull a world to know?

You look across the fruit and flowers,
    My glance your glances find. –
It is our secret, only ours,
    Since all the world is blind.

WASTED DAYS

A fair slim boy not made for this world's pain,
With hair of gold thick clustering round his ears
    And longing eyes half veil'd by foolish tears
Like bluest water seen through mists of rain;
Pale cheeks whereon no kiss hath left its stain,
    Red under-lip drawn in for fear of Love,
    And white throat whiter than the breast of dove –
Alas! alas! If all should be in vain.
Behind, wide fields, and reapers all a-row
In heat and labour toiling wearily,
To no sweet sound of laughter or of lute.
The sun is shooting wide its crimson glow,
Still the boy dreams: nor knows that night is nigh,
And in the night-time no man gathers fruit.

OSCAR WILDE 69

AT THE CAFÉ DOOR

Something they said beside me
made me look toward the café door,
and I saw that lovely body which seemed
as though Eros in his mastery had fashioned it,
joyfully shaping its well-formed limbs,
molding its tall build,
shaping its face tenderly,
and leaving, with a touch of the fingers,
a particular nuance on the brow, the eyes, the lips.

      TRANSLATED BY EDMUND KEELEY AND
      PHILIP SHERRARD

DAYS OF 1908

That year he found himself without a job.
Accordingly he lived by playing cards
and backgammon, and the occasional loan.

A position had been offered in a small
stationer's, at three pounds a month. But he
turned it down unhesitatingly.
It wouldn't do. That was no wage at all
for a sufficiently literate young man of twenty-five.

Two or three shillings a day, won hit or miss –
what could cards and backgammon earn the boy
at *his* kind of working-class café,
however quick his play, however slow his picked
opponents? Worst of all, though, were the loans –
rarely a whole crown, usually half;
sometimes he had to settle for a shilling.

But sometimes for a week or more, set free
from the ghastliness of staying up all night,
he'd cool off with a swim, by morning light.

His clothes by then were in a dreadful state.
He had the one same suit to wear, the one
of much discolored cinnamon.

Ah days of summer, days of nineteen-eight,
excluded from your vision, tastefully,
was that cinnamon-discolored suit.

Your vision preserved him in the very act of
casting it off, throwing it all behind him,
the unfit clothes, the mended underclothing.
Naked he stood, impeccably fair, a marvel –
his hair uncombed, uplifted, his limbs tanned lightly
from those mornings naked at the baths, and at the
        seaside.

72   CONSTANTINE CAVAFY
    TRANSLATED BY JAMES MERRILL

"HAVE YOU HIS LOVELY IMAGE"

Have you his lovely image still in mind,
Who boldly at the chasm's roses caught,
Who passing day forgot in such a find,
Who heavy nectar from the clusters sought?

Who when the sheen of wings had driven him
Too far, for resting turned into the park,
Who musing sat at yonder water's rim
And listened to the deep and secret dark . . .

The swan by falling waters left his stand,
His island built of stones that mosses deck,
And laid within a child's caressing hand,
And delicate – his slender neck.

STEFAN GEORGE   73
TRANSLATED BY CAROL NORTH VALHOPE AND
ERNST MORWITZ

From A SHROPSHIRE LAD

XV

Look not in my eyes, for fear
   They mirror true the sight I see,
And there you find your face too clear
   And love it and be lost like me.
One the long nights through must lie
   Spent in star-defeated sighs,
But why should you as well as I
   Perish? gaze not in my eyes.

A Grecian lad, as I hear tell,
   One that many loved in vain,
Looked into a forest well
   And never looked away again.
There, when the turf in springtime flowers,
   With downward eye and gazes sad,
Stands amid the glancing showers
   A jonquil, not a Grecian lad.

From EPITHALAMION

Hark, hearer, hear what I do; lend a thought now,
    make believe
We are leafwhelmed somewhere with the hood
Of some branchy bunchy bushybowered wood,
Southern dene or Lancashire clough or Devon cleave,
That leans along the loins of hills, where a
    candycoloured, where a gluegold-brown
Marbled river, boisterously beautiful, between
Roots and rocks is danced and dandled, all in froth and
    water-blowballs, down.
We are there, when we hear a shout
That the hanging honeysuck, the dogeared hazels in
    the cover
Makes dither, makes hover
And the riot of a rout
Of, it must be, boys from the town
Bathing: it is summer's sovereign good.

By there comes a listless stranger: beckoned by the noise
He drops towards the river: unseen
Sees the bevy of them, how the boys
With dare and with downdolphinry and bellbright
    bodies huddling out,
Are earthworld, airworld, waterworld thorough
    hurled, all by turn and turn about.

This garland of their gambols flashes in his breast
Into such a sudden zest
Of summertime joys
That he hies to a pool neighbouring; sees it is
    the best
There; sweetest, freshest, shadowiest;
Fairyland; silk-beech, scrolled ash, packed sycamore,
    wild wychelm, hornbeam fretty overstood
By. Rafts and rafts of flake-leaves light, dealt so,
    painted on the air,
Hang as still as hawk or hawkmoth, as the stars or
    as the angels there,
Like the thing that never knew the earth, never
    off roots
Rose. Here he feasts: lovely all is! No more: off
    with – down he dings
His bleachèd both and woolwoven wear:
Careless these in coloured wisp
All lie tumbled-to; then with loop-locks
Forward falling, forehead frowning, lips crisp
Over finger-teasing task, his twiny boots
Fast he opens, last he offwrings
Till walk the world he can with bare his feet
And come where lies a coffer, burly all of blocks
Built of chancequarrièd, selfquainèd rocks
And the water warbles over into, filleted with glassy
    grassy quicksilvery shivès and shoots

And with heavenfallen freshness down from
    moorland still brims,
Dark or daylight on and on. Here he will then, here
    he will the fleet
Flinty kindcold element let break across his limbs
Long. Where we leave him, froliclavish, while he
    looks about him, laughs, swims.

EPISODE OF HANDS

The unexpected interest made him flush.
Suddenly he seemed to forget the pain, –
Consented, – and held out
One finger from the others.

The gash was bleeding, and a shaft of sun
That glittered in and out among the wheels,
Fell lightly, warmly, down into the wound.

And as the fingers of the factory owner's son,
That knew a grip for books and tennis
As well as one for iron and leather, –
As his taut, spare fingers wound the gauze
Around the thick bed of the wound,
His own hands seemed to him
Like wings of butterflies
Flickering in sunlight over summer fields.

The knots and notches, – many in the wide
Deep hand that lay in his, – seemed beautiful.
They were like the marks of wild ponies' play, –
Bunches of new green breaking a hard turf.

And factory sounds and factory thoughts
Were banished from him by that larger, quieter hand
That lay in his with the sun upon it.
And as the bandage knot was tightened
The two men smiled into each other's eyes.

THE COASTGUARD STATION

At dawn, a few recruits have a smoke
on the patio above the breakers;
across the sand path, I sit with my books,
hearing their animal coughs.

Strangely, watching them tranquillizes me.
Their big clapboard house
is illuminated all night,
like the unconscious, though no one enters.
Even in hallucinatory fog,
their pier is flash-bulb bright
and staunch as Abraham.
Overhead, a gull scavenges like a bare hand.
An officer, in orange overalls,
stares like a python
up into the window where I am.

What does it mean to be chosen?
To have your body grow into a hero's
and have done nothing to achieve it?
To seize a birthright, unobstructed?
To dominate with confident bearing?
That is their covenant,
even cold-stupefied and lethargic:
hearing the blessing of Isaac to Jacob.

Naked and a little drunk,
I sit chafing at it,
the nerves in my teeth aching,
lording it over the rest of me.

Why do I appear to be what I am not?
To the world, arrogantly self-sufficient.
To myself, womanish, conflicted, subservient,
like Esau pleading, "Bless me also, Father!"
I hate what I am and I hate what I am not.

LOOKING AT EACH OTHER

Yes, we were looking at each other
Yes, we knew each other very well
Yes, we had made love with each other many times
Yes, we had heard music together
Yes, we had gone to the sea together
Yes, we had cooked and eaten together
Yes, we had laughed often day and night
Yes, we fought violence and knew violence
Yes, we hated the inner and outer oppression
Yes, that day we were looking at each other
Yes, we saw the sunlight pouring down
Yes, the corner of the table was between us
Yes, bread and flowers were on the table
Yes, our eyes saw each other's eyes
Yes, our mouths saw each other's mouth
Yes, our breasts saw each other's breasts
Yes, our bodies entire saw each other
Yes, it was beginning in each
Yes, it threw waves across our lives
Yes, the pulses were becoming very strong
Yes, the beating became very delicate
Yes, the calling   the arousal
Yes, the arriving   the coming
Yes, there it was for both entire
Yes, we were looking at each other

"THE STARS DON'T MOVE"

The stars don't move in the sky,
the summer hour is like any other summer.
But the boy walking ahead of you —
if you don't speak up he'll never be the one ...

LOVING

LOVE THE LIGHT-GIVER
To Tommaso de' Cavalieri

With your fair eyes a charming light I see,
for which my own blind eyes would peer in vain;
stayed by your feet the burden I sustain
which my lame feet find all too strong for me;

wingless upon your pinions forth I fly;
heavenward your spirit stirreth me to strain;
e'en as you will I blush and blanch again,
freeze in the sun, burn 'neath a frosty sky.

Your will includes and is the lord of mine;
life to my thoughts within your heart is given;
my words begin to breathe upon your breath:

like to the moon am I, that cannot shine
alone; for lo! our eyes see nought in heaven
save what the living sun illumineth.

MICHELANGELO BUONARROTI   87
TRANSLATED BY J. A. SYMONDS

STANZAS FOR MUSIC

There be none of Beauty's daughters
    With a magic like thee;
And like music on the waters
    Is thy sweet voice to me:
When, as if its sound were causing
The charmèd ocean's pausing,
The waves lie still and gleaming,
And the lull'd winds seem dreaming.

And the midnight moon is weaving
    Her bright chain o'er the deep;
Whose breast is gently heaving,
    As an infant's asleep:
So the spirit bows before thee,
To listen and adore thee;
With a full but soft emotion,
Like the swell of Summer's ocean.

From ALEXANDRIAN SONGS

Leaving my house in the morning,
I look up at the sun and think:
"How like my love
when he bathes in the river,
or gazes at the distant garden plots!"
And when in the heat of noon I gaze
at the same burning sun,
again you come into my mind, my dearest one:
"How like my love
when he rides through the crowded streets!"
And when I look upon soft sunsets,
it is to you that memory returns,
drowsing, wan from our caresses,
your drooping eyelids shadowed deep.

MIKHAIL KUZMIN   89
TRANSLATED BY MICHAEL GREEN

"WHEN I HEARD AT THE CLOSE
OF THE DAY"

When I heard at the close of the day how my name had
    been receiv'd with plaudits in the capitol, still it
    was not a happy night for me that follow'd,
And else when I carous'd, or when my plans were
    accomplish'd still I was not happy,
But the day when I rose at dawn from the bed of perfect
    health, refresh'd, singing, inhaling the ripe breath
    of autumn,
When I saw the full moon in the west grow pale and
    disappear in the morning light,
When I wander'd alone over the beach, and undressing
    bathed, laughing with the cool waters, and saw
    the sun rise,
And when I thought how my dear friend my lover was
    on his way coming, O then I was happy,
O then each breath tasted sweeter, and all that day my
    food nourish'd me more, and the beautiful day
    pass'd well,
And the next came with equal joy, and with the next at
    evening came my friend,
And that night while all was still I heard the waters
    roll slowly continually up the shores,
I heard the hissing rustle of the liquid and sands as
    directed to me whispering to congratulate me,

For the one I love most lay sleeping by me under the
    same cover in the cool night,
In the stillness in the autumn moonbeams his face was
    inclined toward me,
And his arm lay lightly around my breast – and that
    night I was happy.

"WE TWO BOYS TOGETHER CLINGING"

We two boys together clinging,
One the other never leaving,
Up and down the roads going, North and South
    excursions making,
Power enjoying, elbows stretching, fingers clutching,
Arm'd and fearless, eating, drinking, sleeping, loving,
No law less than ourselves owning, sailing, soldiering,
    thieving, threatening,
Misers, menials, priests alarming, air breathing, water
    drinking, on the turf or the sea-beach dancing,
Cities wrenching, ease scorning, statues mocking,
    feebleness chasing,
Fulfilling our foray.

THE BANDAGED SHOULDER

He said he'd hurt himself against a wall or
    had fallen down.
But there was probably some other reason
for the wounded, the bandaged shoulder.

Because of a rather abrupt gesture,
as he reached for a shelf to bring down
some photographs he wanted to look at,
the bandage came undone and a little blood ran.

I did it up again, taking my time
over the binding; he wasn't in pain
and I liked looking at the blood.
It was a thing of my love, that blood.

When he left, I found, in front of his chair,
a bloody rag, part of the dressing,
a rag to be thrown straight into the garbage;
and I put it to my lips
and kept it there a long while –
the blood of love against my lips.

CONSTANTINE CAVAFY   93
TRANSLATED BY EDMUND KEELEY
AND PHILIP SHERRARD

TWO YOUNG MEN, 23 TO 24 YEARS OLD

He'd been sitting in the café since ten-thirty
expecting him to turn up any minute.
Midnight went by, and he was still waiting for him.
It was now after one-thirty, and the café was
    almost deserted.
He'd grown tired of reading newspapers
mechanically. Of his three lonely shillings
only one was left: waiting that long,
he'd spent the others on coffees and brandy.
He'd smoked all his cigarettes.
So much waiting had worn him out. Because
alone like that for so many hours,
he'd also begun to have disturbing thoughts
about the immoral life he was living.

But when he saw his friend come in —
weariness, boredom, thoughts vanished at once.

His friend brought unexpected news.
He'd won sixty pounds playing cards.

Their good looks, their exquisite youthfulness,
the sensitive love they shared
were refreshed, livened, invigorated
by the sixty pounds from the card table.

Now all joy and vitality, feeling and charm,
they went – not to the homes of their respectable
    families
(where they were no longer wanted anyway) –
they went to a familiar and very special
house of debauchery, and they asked for a bedroom
and expensive drinks, and they drank again.

And when the expensive drinks were finished
and it was close to four in the morning,
happy, they gave themsclves to love.

CONSTANTINE CAVAFY

TRANSLATED BY EDMUND KEELEY

AND PHILIP SHERRARD

SECOND THOUGHTS

I thought of leaving her for a day
In town, it was such iron winter
At Durdans, the garden frosty clay,
The woods as dry as any splinter,
The sky congested. I would break
From the deep, lethargic, country air
To the shining lamps, to the clash of the play,
And to-morrow, wake
Beside her, a thousand things to say.
I planned – O more – I had almost started; –
I lifted her face in my hands to kiss, –
A face in a border of fox's fur,
For the bitter black wind had stricken her,
And she wore it – her soft hair straying out
Where it buttoned against the gray, leather snout:
In an instant we should have parted;
But at sight of the delicate world within
That fox-fur collar, from brow to chin,
At sight of those wonderful eyes from the mine,
Coal pupils, an iris of glittering spa,
And the wild, ironic, defiant shine
As of a creature behind a bar
One has captured, and, when three lives are past,
May hope to reach the heart of at last,
All that, and the love at her lips, combined

To shew me what folly it were to miss
A face with such thousand things to say,
And beside these, such thousand more to spare,
For the shining lamps, for the clash of the play –
O madness; not for a single day
Could I leave her! I stayed behind.

ROSA ROSARUM

Give me, O friend, the secret of thy heart
   Safe in my breast to hide,
So that the leagues which keep our lives apart
   May not ever our souls divide.

Give me the secret of thy life to lay
   Asleep within my own,
Nor dream that it shall mock thee any day
   By any sign or tone.

Nay, as in walking through some convent-close,
   Passing beside a well,
Oft have we thrown a red and scented rose
   To watch it as it fell;

Knowing that never more the rose shall rise
   To shame us, being dead;
Watching it spin and dwindle till it lies
   At rest, a speck of red —

Thus, I beseech thee, down the silent deep
   And darkness of my heart,
Cast thou a rose; give me a rose to keep,
   My friend, before we part.

For, as thou passest down thy garden-ways,
    Many a blossom there
Groweth for thee: lilies and laden bays,
    And rose and lavender.

But down the darking well one only rose
    In all the year is shed;
And o'er that chill and secret wave it throws
    A sudden dawn of red.

VOYAGES, III

Infinite consanguinity it bears –
This tendered theme of you that light
Retrieves from sea plains where the sky
Resigns a breast that every wave enthrones;
While ribboned water lanes I wind
Are laved and scattered with no stroke
Wide from your side, whereto this hour
The sea lifts, also, reliquary hands.

And so, admitted through black swollen gates
That must arrest all distance otherwise, –
Past whirling pillars and lithe pediments,
Light wrestling there incessantly with light,
Star kissing star through wave on wave unto
Your body rocking!
               and where death, if shed,
Presumes no carnage, but this single change, –
Upon the steep floor flung from dawn to dawn
The silken skilled transmemberment of song;

Permit me voyage, love, into your hands ...

"SINCE THE FIRST TOSS OF GALE"

Since the first toss of gale that blew
Me in to you
The wind that our still love awakened
Has never slackened,
But watchful with nightfall keeps pace
With each embrace.
If we love out the winter, my dear,
This will be a year
That babes now lulled on arm will quote
With rusty throat.
For long meeting of our lips
Shall be breaking of ships,
For breath drawn quicker men drowned
And trees downed.
Throe shall fell roof-tree, pulse's knock
Undermine rock,
A cry hurl seas against the land,
A raiding hand,
Scattering lightning along thighs
Lightning from skies
Wrench, and fierce sudden snows clamp deep
On earth our sleep.
Yet who would guess our coming together
Should breed wild weather
Who saw us now? – with looks as sure

As the demure
Flame of our candle, no more plied
By tempest outside
Than those deep ocean weeds unrecking
What winds, what wrecking
What wrath of wild our dangerous peace
Waits to release.

"THE EYES OF THE BODY, BEING BLINDFOLD BY NIGHT"

The eyes of the body, being blindfold by night
Refer to the eyes of mind – at brain's command
Study imagination's map, then order out a hand
To journey forth as deputy for sight.

Thus and by these ordered ways
I come at you – Hand deft and delicate
To trace the suavely laid and intricate
Route of your body's maze.

My hand, being deft and delicate, displays
Unerring judgment; cleaves between your thighs
Clean, as a ray-directed airplane flies.

Thus I, within these strictly ordered ways,
Although blindfolded, seize with more than sight
Your moonlit meadows and your shadowed night.

"WHEN I HAVE SAID"

When I have said "I love you" I have said
Nothing at all to tell you; I cannot find
Any speech in any country of the mind
Which might inform you whither I have fled.
In saying "I love you" I have gone so far
Away from you, into so strange a land;
You may not find me, may not understand
How I am exiled, driven to a star

Till now deserted. Here I stand about,
Eat, sleep, bewail, feel lonely and explore,
Remember how I loved the world, before,
Tremble in case that memory lets me out.
Islanded here, I wait for you to come —
Waiting the day that exiles you to home.

EVENING SONG

Dear love, what thing of all the things that be
Is ever worth one thought from you or me,
    Save only Love,
    Save only Love?

The days so short, the nights so quick to flee,
The world so wide, so deep and dark the sea,
    So dark the sea;

So far the suns and every listless star,
Beyond their light – Ah! dear, who knows how far,
    Who knows how far?

One thing of all dim things I know is true,
The heart within me knows, and tells it you,
    And tells it you.

So blind is life, so long at last is sleep,
And none but Love to bid us laugh or weep,
    And none but Love,
    And none but Love.

"FISH IN THE UNRUFFLED LAKES"

Fish in the unruffled lakes
Their swarming colours wear,
Swans in the winter air
A white perfection have,
And the great lion walks
Through his innocent grove;
Lion, fish and swan
Act, and are gone
Upon Time's toppling wave.

We, till shadowed days are done,
We must weep and sing
Duty's conscious wrong,
The Devil in the clock,
The goodness carefully worn
For atonement or for luck;
We must lose our loves,
On each beast and bird that moves
Turn an envious look.

Sighs for folly done and said
Twist our narrow days,
But I must bless, I must praise
That you, my swan, who have
All gifts that to the swan

106

Impulsive Nature gave,
The majesty and pride,
Last night should add
Your voluntary love.

LULLABY

Lay your sleeping head, my love,
Human on my faithless arm;
Time and fevers burn away
Individual beauty from
Thoughtful children, and the grave
Proves the child ephemeral:
But in my arms till break of day
Let the living creature lie,
Mortal, guilty, but to me
The entirely beautiful.

Soul and body have no bounds:
To lovers as they lie upon
Her tolerant enchanted slope
In their ordinary swoon,
Grave the vision Venus sends
Of supernatural sympathy,
Universal love and hope;
While an abstract insight wakes
Among the glaciers and the rocks
The hermit's carnal ecstasy.

Certainty, fidelity
On the stroke of midnight pass
Like vibrations of a bell

And fashionable madmen raise
Their pedantic boring cry:
Every farthing of the cost,
All the dreaded cards foretell,
Shall be paid, but from this night
Not a whisper, not a thought,
Not a kiss nor look be lost.

Beauty, midnight, vision dies:
Let the winds of dawn that blow
Softly round your dreaming head
Such a day of welcome show
Eye and knocking heart may bless,
Find our mortal world enough;
Noons of dryness find you fed
By the involuntary powers,
Nights of insult let you pass
Watched by every human love.

I GET A KICK OUT OF YOU

I get no kick from champagne.
Mere alcohol doesn't thrill me at all,
So tell me why should it be true
That I get a kick out of you?
Some get a kick from cocaine.
I'm sure that if I took even one sniff
That would bore me terrific'ly too
Yet I get a kick out of you.
I get a kick ev'ry time I see
You standing there before me.
I get a kick though it's clear to me
You obviously don't adore me.
I get no kick in a plane.
Flying too high with some guy in the sky
Is my idea of nothing to do,
Yet I get a kick out of you.

BUNDLES FOR THEM

We were able to notice that each one in a way carried a bundle, they were not a trouble to them nor were they all bundles as some of them were chickens some of them pheasants some of them sheep and some of them bundles, they were not a trouble to them and then indeed we learned that it was the principal recreation and they were so arranged that they were not given away, and to-day they were given away.

I will not look at them again.

They will not look for them again.

They have not seen them here again.

They are in there and we hear them again.

In which way are stars brighter than they are. When we have come to this decision. We mention many thousands of buds. And when I close my eyes I see them.

If you hear her snore

It is not before you love her

You love her so that to be her beau is very lovely

She is sweetly there and her curly hair is very lovely

She is sweetly here and I am very near and that is very lovely.

She is my tender sweet and her little feet are stretched out well which is a treat and very lovely

Her little tender nose is between her little eyes which close and are very lovely.

She is very lovely and mine which is very lovely.

WAITING

What reasons may the single heart employ
When, forward and impervious, it moves
Through savage times and science toward the joy
Of love's next meeting in a threatened space?
What privilege is this, whose tenure gives
One anesthetic hour of release,
While the air raid's spattered signature displays
A bitter artistry among the trees?

Thus, in our published era, sweetness lives
And keeps its reasons in a private room;
As, in the hothouse, white hibiscus proves
A gardener's thesis all the winter through,
So does this tenderness of waiting bloom
Like tropics under glass, my dear, for you.

RAIN TOWARDS MORNING

The great light cage has broken up in the air,
freeing, I think, about a million birds
whose wild ascending shadows will not be back,
and all the wires come falling down.
No cage, no frightening birds; the rain
is brightening now. The face is pale
that tried the puzzle of their prison
and solved it with an unexpected kiss,
whose freckled unsuspected hands alit.

THE SHAMPOO

The still explosions on the rocks,
the lichens, grow
by spreading, gray, concentric shocks.
They have arranged
to meet the rings around the moon, although
within our memories they have not changed.

And since the heavens will attend
as long on us,
you've been, dear friend,
precipitate and pragmatical;
and look what happens. For Time is
nothing if not amenable.

The shooting stars in your black hair
in bright formation
are flocking where,
so straight, so soon?
– Come, let me wash it in this big tin basin,
battered and shiny like the moon.

DAYS OF 1964

Houses, an embassy, the hospital,
Our neighborhood sun-cured if trembling still
In pools of the night's rain ...
Across the street that led to the center of town
A steep hill kept one company part way
Or could be climbed in twenty minutes
For some literally breathtaking views,
Framed by umbrella pines, of city and sea.
Underfoot, cyclamen, autumn crocus grew
Spangled as with fine sweat among the relics
Of good times had by all. If not Olympus,
An out-of-earshot, year-round hillside revel.

I brought home flowers from my climbs.
Kyria Kleo who cleaned for us
Put them in water, sighing *Virgin, Virgin.*
Her legs hurt. She wore brown, was fat, past fifty,
And looked like a Palmyra matron
Copied in lard and horsehair. How she loved
You, me, loved us all, the bird, the cat!
I think now she *was* love. She sighed and glistened
All day with it, or pain, or both.
(We did not notably communicate.)
She lived nearby with her pious mother
And wastrel son. She called me her real son.

I paid her generously, I dare say.
Love makes one generous. Look at us. We'd known
Each other so briefly that instead of sleeping
We lay whole nights, open, in the lamplight,
And gazed, or traded stories.

One hour comes back – you gasping in my arms
With love, or laughter, or both,
I having just remembered and told you
What I'd looked up to see on my way downtown at noon:
Poor old Kleo, her aching legs,
Trudging into the pines. I called,
Called three times before she turned.
Above a tight, skyblue sweater, her face
Was painted. Yes. Her face was painted
Clown-white, white of the moon by daylight,
Lidded with pearl, mouth a poinsettia leaf,
Eat me, pay me – the erotic mask
Worn the world over by illusion
To weddings of itself and simple need.

Startled mute, we had stared – was love illusion? –
And gone our ways. Next, I was crossing a square
In which a moveable outdoor market's
Vegetables, chickens, pottery kept materializing
Through a dream-press of hagglers each at heart
Leery lest he be taken, plucked,

The bird, the flower of that November mildness,
Self lost up soft clay paths, or found, foothold,
Where the bud throbs awake
The better to be nipped, self on its knees in mud –
Here I stopped cold, for both our sakes;

And calmer on my way home bought us fruit.

Forgive me if you read this. (And may Kyria Kleo,
Should someone ever put it into Greek
And read it aloud to her, forgive me, too.)
I had gone so long without loving,
I hardly knew what I was thinking.

Where I hid my face, your touch, quick, merciful,
Blindfolded me. A god breathed from my lips.
If that was illusion, I wanted it to last long;
To dwell, for its daily pittance, with us there,
Cleaning and watering, sighing with love or pain.
I hoped it would climb when it needed to the heights
Even of degradation, as I for one
Seemed, those days, to be always climbing
Into a world of wild
Flowers, feasting, tears – or was I falling, legs
Buckling, heights, depths,
Into a pool of each night's rain?
But you were everywhere beside me, masked,
As who was not, in laughter, pain, and love.

LIVING TOGETHER

Of you I have no memory, keep no promise.
But, as I read, drink, wait, and watch the surf,
Faithful, almost forgotten, your demand
Becomes all others, and this loneliness
The need that is your presence. In the dark,
Beneath the lamp, attentive, like a sound
I listen for, you draw near – closer, surer
Than speech, or sight, or love, or love returned.

EVESONG

My love takes an apple to bed
apple, apple she puts the bite on you
or drops you, irresistible, to halt my chase.
As I pick you up and consider
your shape, texture
your virgin unblushed green
she is gone over the dream horizon
while I labour after with this
core, kore, mon cœur, half eaten
bitten fingernail of a poem
going down with the moon
these pips my teeth crack
for a taste of
bittersweet as almond skinned
cleft and dimpled
the apples she brings to bed

TO YOU

What is more beautiful than night
and someone in your arms
that's what we love about art
it seems to prefer us and stays

if the moon or a gasping candle
sheds a little light or even dark
you become a landscape in a landscape
with rocks and craggy mountains

and valleys full of sweaty ferns
breathing and lifting into the clouds
which have actually come low
as a blanket of aspirations' blue

for once not a melancholy color
because it is looking back at us
there's no need for vistas we are one
in the complicated foreground of space

the architects are most courageous
because it stands for all to see
and for a long time just as
the words "I'll always love you"

impulsively appear in the dark sky
and we are happy and stick by them
like a couple of painters in neon allowing
the light to glow there over the river

HAVING A COKE WITH YOU

is even more fun than going to San Sebastian, Irún,
     Hendaye, Biarritz, Bayonne
or being sick to my stomach on the Travesera de
     Gracia in Barcelona
partly because in your orange shirt you look like a
     better happier St Sebastian
partly because of my love for you, partly because of
     your love for yoghurt
partly because of the fluorescent orange tulips around
     the birches
partly because of the secrecy our smiles take on before
     people and statuary
it is hard to believe when I'm with you that there can
     be anything as still
as solemn as unpleasantly definitive as statuary when
     right in front of it
in the warm New York 4 o'clock light we are drifting
     back and forth
between each other like a tree breathing through its
     spectacles

and the portrait show seems to have no faces in it at all,
     just paint

you suddenly wonder why in the world anyone ever
    did them
               I look
at you and I would rather look at you than all the
    portraits in the world
except possibly for the *Polish Rider* occasionally and
    anyway it's in the Frick
which thank heavens you haven't gone to yet so we can
    go together the first time
and the fact that you move so beautifully more or less
    takes care of Futurism
just as at home I never think of the *Nude Descending a
    Staircase* or
at a rehearsal a single drawing of Leonardo or
    Michelangelo that used to wow me
and what good does all the research of the
    Impressionists do them
when they never got the right person to stand near the
    tree when the sun sank
or for that matter Marino Marini when he didn't pick
    the rider as carefully as the horse
        it seems they were all cheated of some
    marvellous experience
which is not going to go wasted on me which is why
    I'm telling you about it

NIGHT GLEAM

Over and over thru the dull material world the call is
      made
over and over thru the dull material world I make the
      call
O English folk, in Sussex night, thru black beech tree
      branches
the full moon shone at three AM, I stood in under wear
      on the lawn –
I saw a mustached English man I loved, athlete's breast
      and farmer's arms,
I lay in bed that night many loves beating in my heart
sleepless hearing songs of generations returning
      intelligent memory
to my frame, and so went to dwell again in my heart
and worship the Lovers there, love's teachers, youths
      and poets who live forever
in the secret heart, in the dark night, in the full moon,
      year after year
over & over thru the dull material world the call is
      made.

POEM

Your enchantment
enchains me, stretched
out there, planked
like a steak or
a shad in season.
And there, where
you flower there.
You're cool to my
touch, soon growing
warm, smooth but not
sleek. I love you
too much? Not quite
possible. The thought
of harm from you is
far from me as those
Vermont hills, en-
flamed, in October,
as I by you, in their
seasonal rush. To
go up in leaves! I
wish I could, as I
sink down beside you.

TREE MARRIAGE

In Chota Nagpur and Bengal
the betrothed are tied with threads to
mango trees, they marry the trees
as well as one another, and
the two trees marry each other.
Could we do that some time with oaks
or beeches? This gossamer we
hold each other with, this web
of love and habit is not enough.
In mistrust of heavier ties,
I would like tree-siblings for us,
standing together somewhere, two
trees married with us, lightly, their
fingers barely touching in sleep,
our threads invisible but holding.

A LIGHT LEFT ON

In the evening we came back
Into our yellow room,
For a moment taken aback
To find the light left on,
Falling on silent flowers
Table, book, empty chair
While we had gone elsewhere,
Had been away for hours.

When we came home together
We found the inside weather.
All of our love unended
The quiet light demanded,
And we gave, in a look
At yellow walls and open book.
The deepest world we share
And do not talk about
But have to have, was there,
And by that light found out.

MAY SARTON   127

"WAKING, I ALWAYS WAKED
YOU AWAKE"

Waking, I always waked you awake
As always I fell from the ledge of your arms
Into the soft sand and silt of sleep
Permitted by you awake, with your arms firm.

Waking, always I waked immediately
To the face you were when I was off sleeping,
Ribboned with sea weed or running with deer
In a valentine country of swans in the door.

Waking, always waked to the tasting of dew
As if my sleep issued tears for its loving
Waking, always waked, swimming from foam
Breathing from mountains clad in a cloud.

As waking, always waked in the health of your eyes,
Curled your leaf hair, uncovered your hands,
Good morning like birds in an innocence
Wild as the Indies we ever first found.

NEITHER WANTING MORE

To lie with you
in a field of grass
to lie there forever
and let time pass

Touching lightly
shoulder and thigh
Neither wanting more
Neither asking why

To have your whole
cool body's length
along my own
to know the strength
of a secret tide
of longing seep
into our veins
go deep ... deep

Dissolving flesh
and melting bone
Oh to lie with you
alone

To feel your breast
rise with my sigh
To hold you mirrored
in my eye

Neither wanting more
Neither asking why

THE OASIS

I thought I held a fruit cupped in my hand.
Its sweetness burst
And loosed its juice. After long traveling,
After so long a thirst,
> I asked myself: Is this a drought-born dream?
> It was no dream.

I thought I slipped into a hidden room
Out of harsh light.
In cushioned dark, among rich furnishings,
There I restored my sight.
> Such luxury could never be for me!
> It was for me.

I thought I touched a mind that fitted mine
As bodies fit,
Angle to curve; and my mind throbbed to feel
The pulsing of that wit.
> This comes too late, I said. It can't be true!
> But it was true.

I thought the desert ended, and I felt
The fountains leap.
Then gratitude could answer gratitude
Till sleep entwined with sleep.
> Despair once cried: No passion's left inside!
> It lied. It lied.

NAOMI REPLANSKY   131

THE PEOPLE'S HOTEL

And afterwards he said please
empty your pockets: handful
of keys and small change he spent
quiet minutes sketching.
An astonishment, where instead
of one large coin the moon appeared,
familiar, rayed and bruised,
face of a loved one gone
to ruin. He pushed it toward me,
stood to go, asking for nothing
more than that we meet again.

DOMESTICITIES

We ate from the dish of eyes
and as eyes met, making out
light by darkness, we hungered:
      the dish is a questioning of the dish.

We drank from the cup of hands
and as hands met, reaching down
for what was up, we thirsted:
      the cup is a questioning of the cup.

We slept in the bed of flesh
and as flesh met, melting back
to the lost action, we kept
      forgiving, and for good: no questions asked.

THE HUG

It was your birthday, we had drunk and dined
　　Half of the night with our old friend
　　　　Who'd showed us in the end
　　To a bed I reached in one drunk stride.
　　　　Already I lay snug,
And drowsy with the wine dozed on one side.

I dozed, I slept. My sleep broke on a hug,
　　　　Suddenly, from behind,
In which the full lengths of our bodies pressed:
　　　　Your instep to my heel,
　　My shoulder-blades against your chest.
　　It was not sex, but I could feel
　　The whole strength of your body set,
　　　　　Or braced, to mine,
　　　　And locking me to you
　　As if we were still twenty-two
　　When our grand passion had not yet
　　　　Become familial.
　　My quick sleep had deleted all
　　Of intervening time and place.
　　　　I only knew
The stay of your secure firm dry embrace.

From TWENTY-ONE LOVE POEMS

II

I wake up in your bed. I know I have been dreaming.
Much earlier, the alarm broke us from each other,
you've been at your desk for hours. I know what I
     dreamed:
our friend the poet comes into my room
where I've been writing for days,
drafts, carbons, poems are scattered everywhere,
and I want to show her one poem
which is the poem of my life. But I hesitate,
and wake. You've kissed my hair
to wake me. *I dreamed you were a poem,*
I say, *a poem I wanted to show someone* . . .
and I laugh and fall dreaming again
of the desire to show you to everyone I love,
to move openly together
in the pull of gravity, which is not simple,
which carries the feathered grass a long way down
     the upbreathing air.

From TWENTY-ONE LOVE POEMS

III

Since we're not young, weeks have to do time
for years of missing each other. Yet only this odd warp
in time tells me we're not young.
Did I ever walk the morning streets at twenty,
my limbs streaming with a purer joy?
did I lean from any window over the city
listening for the future
as I listen here with nerves tuned for your ring?
And you, you move toward me with the same tempo.
Your eyes are everlasting, the green spark
of the blue-eyed grass of early summer,
the green-blue wild cress washed by the spring.
At twenty, yes: we thought we'd live forever.
At forty-five, I want to know even our limits.
I touch you knowing we weren't born tomorrow,
and somehow, each of us will help the other live,
and somewhere, each of us must help the other die.

From TWENTY-ONE LOVE POEMS

XVI

Across a city from you, I'm with you,
just as an August night
moony, inlet-warm, seabathed, I watched you sleep,
the scrubbed, sheenless wood of the dressing-table
cluttered with our brushes, books, vials in the
     moonlight –
or a salt-mist orchard, lying at your side
watching red sunset through the screendoor of
     the cabin,
G minor Mozart on the tape-recorder,
falling asleep to the music of the sea.
This island of Manhattan is wide enough
for both of us, and narrow:
I can hear your breath tonight, I know how your face
lies upturned, the halflight tracing
your generous, delicate mouth
where grief and laughter sleep together.

LOVE POEM

Speak earth and bless me
with what is richest
make sky flow honey out of my hips
rigid as mountains
spread over a valley
carved out by the mouth of rain

And I knew when I entered her   I was
high wind in her forest's hollow
fingers whispering sound
honey flowed   from the split cut
impaled on a lance of tongues
on the tips of her breasts   on her navel
and my breath   howling into her entrances
through lungs of pain.

Greedy as herring-gulls
or a child
I swing out over   the earth
over and over   again.

KEEPING TIME

This night so gently
we circle the clock of streets.
I hear your feet before we meet,
I've come empty like this before.
My mouth parched on "hello"
fracturing me inside, my eyes
blurring like seaglass
at other faces you've shown.

So come with me again.
What we call ourselves they have
no names for, nor the peeled

fruit offered between us.
And with lips round in even
cadence, we shall recall
this night so gently.

THE ROMAN BATHS AT NÎMES

In the hall of mirrors nobody speaks.
An ember smolders before hollowed cheeks.
Someone empties pockets, loose change and keys,
into a locker. My god, forgive me.
Some say love, disclosed, repels what it sees,
yet if I touch the darkness, it touches me.
In the steamroom, inconsolable tears
fall against us. In the whirlpool, my arms,
rowing through little green crests, help to steer
the body, riding against death. Yet what harm
is there in us? I swear to you, my friend,
crossarmed in a bright beach towel, turning round
to see my face in lamplight, that eye, ear
and tongue, good things, make something sweet
        of fear.

"AH, LOVE, YOU SMELL OF PETROLEUM"

Ah, Love, you smell of petroleum
and overwork
with grease on your fingernails,
paint in your hair
there is a pained look in your eye
from no appreciation
you speak to me of the lilacs
and appleblossoms we ought to have
the banquets we should be serving,
afterwards rubbing each other for hours
with tenderness and genuine
olive oil
someday. Meantime here is your cracked plate
with spaghetti. Wash your hands &
touch me, praise
my cooking. I shall praise your calluses,
we shall dance in the kitchen of our imagination.

BLACK BEANS

Times are lean,
Pretty Baby,
the beans are burnt
to the bottom
of the battered pot.
Let's make fierce love
on the overstuffed,
hand-me-down sofa.
We can burn it up, too.
Our hungers
will evaporate like – money.
I smell your lust,
not the pot burnt black
with tonight's meager meal.
So we can't buy flowers
for our table.
Our kisses are petals,
our tongues caress the bloom.
Who dares to tell us
we are poor and powerless?
We keep treasure
any king would count as dear.
Come on, Pretty Baby.
Our souls can't be crushed
like cats crossing streets too soon.

Let the beans burn all night long.
Our chipped water glasses are filled
with wine from our loving.
And the burnt black beans –
caviar.

FABLE

It was early fall. You rowed me
around the pond
in your ancient boat.
Tart apples lay in a bag with the cheese.
I read you a story
about two women who could not stop
touching each other.
Trumpeter swans paddled close
and you tossed hard French bread
at their black beaks. When you got cold
I gave you my jacket, the leather glistened
like a delicate skin
moving through trees.
You let the oars float
in the oarlocks; you let the boat
drift in circles. You let the women
from the story climb
into the boat. I could not
stop staring. Soon their desire
took up so much room we had to throw
the apples overboard. We had to sit cramped
at one end. Finally we just waded in
and hauled the skiff and the women
to the pier. The story got wet.
The pond was a dark wound.

You unlocked the car and touched
my back, a kindness, as if
I'd always been your lover.

POEM #6 FOR b.b.L.

One room away you sleep or do not wake
to any summons love might make
in competition with all hummingbirds/
those wings of utmost stutter
at the starting source
for rapture

infinitesimal
I take away the noise the words
that might disturb
or curb
your flight
and think how you will
curling
pearl into the night
with all my world
at stake

NO KINGDOM

So little wakes you – why
should a little rain,
or my leaving

to stand under it
and naked
because I can,

all neighbors down,
at last down,
for the dreaming, and

every wasp – daily, the yard's
plague – gone,
returned to

whatever shingle or board
roofs their now
thrumless heliport.

Tremblefoot,
mumbler,
you've left

your glass on the porch-railing
– neglect, as
what is fragile, seen

through,
but not at this hour empty:
the way disease does

the body, the way desire
can, or how God
is said to,

slowly rain fills the glass.
Never mind
that no kingdom was ever won

by small gestures:
I'm tipping the rainwater out.
The glass I'll put

here, where you'll find it.

BREATHING YOU IN

The scent you say is no scent
rises from warm ports
between neck and shoulder.
Scent that isn't
witch hazel, vetiver, camphor,
lemon, but is just your skin,
raises a breeze on mine, unpredicted
as freshness I found in woods
where a few blond leaves hung from twigs.
Sweet sharpness,
scent of something still to come,
something soaked in –
chlorine on the cedar deck your thigh presses,
foot drifting in water,
eyes yellow amber behind closed lids.
Soaked in like sun
in the river whose cold silk
wrapped your body in August,
opened dark folds around you.
Closed, opened, around you.

REVISITING THE HAIGHT

That year, sea-fog in tufted hanks
spun through the eucalyptus tops
below our attic flat,
thick coiling strands that looked as if
they passed right through the limbs – intact –
torn along the Panhandle toward the Bay
in the wet salt wind as though

mist and branches inhabited
worlds separate as that warm room was
from the winter weeks outside:
only damp darkening the leaves
at first, to show the two had touched,
and then the fogbank lowered, settling over
their slippery, peeling trunks.

Parchment scraps of their bark littered
the summer grass this afternoon
where I walked, looking up
five stories through those windows, trying
again to bring nearer to mind
two friends I lived with there twelve years ago,
and caught a glimpse, instead,

of a self I'd barely recognized
in our company of dwindled figures
rushing out of sight
as I saw that in twelve more years
torn along in the same wind
with every solid thing today housing my life,
this insight, too,

will shrink and darken to another
almost unrecognizable story.
The shock was like the moment
when last month's earthquake had kept up
long enough to let me watch
the walls and wonder if they'd crack, break open,
fall – then longer, enough

to know myself helpless, freed
from fearing a titanic power
so far beyond my stature
it was without design. I think
that's what I wanted, last night
in your arms – to be caught up beyond design
and sheltered in that wind:

hidden, escaping, safely and well
lost to all but our limbs and glances
tangling till near dawn
– and instead, slowly discovering,
inside the moments our attentive
pleasures open into immensity,
my small self meeting yours.

THE ABSENT-MINDED LOVER'S APOLOGY

I would like you to think I love you *warmly*
Like brown cat yawning among sheets in the linen-
 cupboard.

I would like you to think I love you *resourcefully*
Like rooftop starlings posting chuckles down the flue.

I would like you to think I love you *extravagantly*
Like black cat embracing the floor when you pick up
 the tin opener.

I would like you to think I love you *accurately*
Like Baskerville kern that fits its place to a T.

I would like you to think I love you *with hurrahs and
 hallelujahs*
Like dog whippeting at you down the intricate hillside.

I would like you to think I love you *wittily*
Like pottery Cox that lurks in the fruit-bowl under the
 Granny Smiths.

I would like you to think I love you *pacifically and
    for ever*
Like collared doves on the whitebeam's domestic
    branch.

I would like you to think I love you *chronically*
Like second hand solemnly circumnavigating
    the clock.

And O I want to love you, not in the absent tense,
    but in the here and the now
Like a present-minded lover.

THE FOOD OF LOVE

I could never sing. In the grade-school operetta
I sat dark offstage and clattered coconut shells.
I was the cavalry coming, unmusical, lonely.

For five years I played the piano and metronome.
I read *Deerslayer* in small print while I waited for my
    lesson,
and threw up after the recital at the Leopold Hotel.

I went to a liberal college, but I never learned
how to sit on the floor or help the sweet folk song
    forward.
My partridge had lice, and its pear-tree had cut-worm
    blight.

Yet this song is for you. In your childhood a clear falsetto,
now you sing along in the bars, naming old songs for me.
Even drunk, you chirrup; birds branch in your every
    voice.

It's for you, what I never sing. So I hope if ever
you reach, in the night, for a music that is not there
because you need food, or philosophy, or bail,

you'll remember to hear the noise that a man might make
if he were an amateur, clattering coconut shells,
if he were the cavalry, tone-deaf but on its way.

WILLIAM DICKEY   155

ECSTASY

From LIFTING BELLY (II)

Kiss my lips. She did.
Kiss my lips again she did.
Kiss my lips over and over and over again she did.
I have feathers.
Gentle fishes.
Do you think about apricots. We find them very
    beautiful. It is not alone their colour it is their
    seeds that charm us. We find it a change.
Lifting belly is so strange.
I came to speak about it.
Selected raisins well their grapes grapes are good.
Change your name.
Question and garden.
It's raining. Don't speak about it.
My baby is a dumpling. I want to tell her something.
Wax candles. We have bought a great many
    wax candles. Some are decorated. They have not
    been lighted.
I do not mention roses.
Exactly.
Actually.
Question and butter.
I find the butter very good.
Lifting belly is so kind.
Lifting belly fattily.

Doesn't that astonish you.
You did want me.
Say it again.
Strawberry.
Lifting beside belly.
Lifting kindly belly.
Sing to me I say.

"I LOVE YOU FOR BEING WEAK"

I love you for being weak and coaxing in my arms
And for searching the sure refuge of my arms
Like a warm cradle where you can rest.

I love you for being red-haired like autumn,
Frail image of the Goddess of autumn
Lit up and crowned by the setting sun.

I love you for being slow and walking without a sound
And for talking softly and hating loud sounds,
As one does in the presence of night.

And I love you above all for being frail and faint,
And for moaning with frail sobs of dying,
In the cruel pleasure that persists and torments.

O sister of the Queens of yore, I love to see you,
Exiled in the midst of the splendors of yore,
Whiter than a reflection of moon on lilies.

I love you for not being alarmed, when ashen
And trembling I cannot hide my own ashen face,
O you that will never know how much I love you!

RENÉE VIVIEN   161
TRANSLATED BY SANDIA BELGRADE

WOUNDS OF LOVE

This light, this fire that devours,
this gray landscape that surrounds me,
this pain that comes from one idea,
this anguish of the sky, the earth, the hour,

and this lament of blood that decorates
a pulseless lyre, a lascivious torch,
this burden of the sea that beats upon me,
this scorpion that dwells within my breast

are all a wreath of love, bed of one wounded,
where, sleepless, I dream of your presence
amid the ruins of my fallen breast.

And though I seek the summit of discretion,
your heart gives me a valley spread below
with hemlock and passion of bitter wisdom.

162   FEDERICO GARCÍA LORCA
      TRANSLATED BY JOHN K. WALSH AND
      FRANCISCO ARAGON

THE TORSO

Most beautiful!   the red-flowering eucalyptus,
   the madrone, the yew

Is he ...

So thou wouldst smile, and take me in thine arms
The sight of London to my exiled eyes
Is as Elysium to a new-come soul

If he be Truth
I would dwell in the illusion of him

His hands unlocking from chambers of my male body

such an idea in man's image

rising tides that sweep me towards him

... homosexual?

and at the treasure of his mouth

pour forth my soul

his soul   commingling

I thought a Being more than vast, His body leading
   into Paradise,   his eyes

    quickening a fire in me,   a trembling

   hieroglyph: At the root of the neck

the clavicle, for the neck is the stem of the great
   artery upward into his head that is beautiful

                At the rise of the pectoral muscle,

the nipples, for the breasts are like sleeping fountains
   of feeling in man, waiting above the beat of his
   heart, shielding the rise and fall of his breath, to
   be awakened

                At the axis of his midriff

the navel, for in the pit of his stomach the chord from
   which first he was fed has its temple

                At the root of the groin

the pubic hair, for the torso is the stem in which the
   man flowers forth and leads to the stamen of flesh
   in which his seed rises

a wave of need and desire over   taking me

            cried out my name

        (This was long ago.   It was another life)

                      and said,

        What do you want of me?

I do not know, I said.   I have fallen in love.   He
    has brought me into heights and depths my heart
        would fear   without him.   His look

    pierces my side • fire eyes •

   I have been waiting for you, he said:
              I know what you desire

     you do not yet know   but through me •

And I am with you everywhere.   In your falling

I have fallen from a high place.   I have raised myself

     from darkness in your   rising

                    wherever you are

    my hand in your hand   seeking   the locks, the keys

I am there.   Gathering me, you gather

        your Self •

    For my Other is not a woman but a man

    the King upon whose bosom let me lie.

A PHOTOGRAPH

shows you in a London
room: books, a painting,
your smile, a silky
tie, a suit. And more.
It looks so like you
and I see it every day
(here, on my desk)
which I don't you. Last
Friday night was grand.
We went out, we came
back, we went wild. You
slept. Me too. The pup
woke you and you dressed
and walked him. When
you left, I was sleeping.
When I woke there was
just time to make the
train to a country dinner
and talk about ecstasy.
Which I think comes in
two sorts: that which you
know "Now I'm ecstatic"
like my strange scream
last Friday night. And
another kind, that you

know only in retrospect:
"Why, that joy I felt
and didn't think about
when his feet were in
my lap, or when I looked
down and saw his slanty
eyes shut, that too was
ecstasy. Nor is there
necessarily a downer from
it." Do I believe in
the perfectibility of
man? Strangely enough,
(I've known un-
happiness enough) I′
do. I mean it,
I really do believe
future generations can
live without the in-
tervals of anxious
fear we know between our
bouts and strolls of
ecstasy. The struck ball
finds the pocket. You
smile some years back
in London, I have
known ecstasy and calm:
haven't you, too? Let's

try to understand, my
handsome friend who
wears his nose awry.

1.
she held the flower cold up against her cheek
bones in the dark the petals flattened cold up
against her cheekbones this flower your
fingers you had danced with this flower in your
mouth your tongue had been pink like a cat's
tongue and slender touching the petals you had
danced with this flower in your mouth held in
your teeth your teeth biting the petals the
petals cold up against her cheekbones she held
the flower cold up against her cheekbones in
the dark.

4.
wet earth to my lips
i sing
o and to touch her breasts with gentle fingers
o and to touch
      slant-fingered
      o
      and to touch slant-thrill-fingered
      her warm breasts

i weep to o wet earth and my fingers
where my fingers sing
ohgodohgodohgodohgodohgodohgod

SHENANDOAH

Photograph: Breakfast after our first full night:
Elbow on the table, fist against your face, intent
   on the cup you look into. Your hair glints
     in three-year-old light.
In these rooms of borrowed furniture, white
walls, wide windows that curve, I have been solitary.
   A cymbedium orchid. Artichokes. Fresh
     trout. I tear pink netting from
the orchid, float it. Red wine is breathing. A plane
lands hours away, and I can think of you driving
   a valley roofed with clouds, your voice
     like the charge of new weather.

Yesterday, eyes shut, sun on my face, I could
remember you viscerally: Heat, sun that caressed
   our naked skin, blond grasses, weeds baked
     to vivid rust. There was no
snow – odd that far north in late October. From ours
other mountains were feathery with bare trees
   and some phenomenon of light turned
     their billowing crests
lavender. See those mountains make a giant sprawled
on her back: those, breasts; the one called Otter, torso.
   See the lake bright near her cheek, the
     trout stream etch her chin.

I am afraid in the vestibule, your face
smiling its guileless welcome. I want to cry, hold you,
   open through your breasts into safe billowing
      darkness. I kiss you
as if we are just friends. I lead you through
white rooms. I hand you the orchid because I cannot
   tell you. You reach. I start, as if your touch were
      too much light, I trim
the artichokes. The red wine breathes. I must cover
the curved windows. In this valley roofed with clouds,
   I live
   alone in rooms on a street where
      all the shades are pulled.

We drink red wine. We unbutton, touch. We eat
trout — clouded eye, clear black night shut from the
      house, petal
   flush of your skin. We eat artichokes, mark
      leaf after leaf with our teeth.
The orchid floats. It is your darkness I want with my
mouth. If I could speak as sound not edged into
   word, I could tell you. Leaves now: two, four,
      five at once. We reach
center, loose lavender-streaked swirl, split the naked
heart in the night bed where I speak with my hands
   and we breathe, mouth to mouth, unedged,
      shorn to simple tenderness.

PEONIES

Ample creamy heads beaten down vulgarly,
as if by some deeply sado-masochistic impulse,
like the desire to subdue, which is normal and active,
and the desire for suffering, which is not;
papery white featherings stapled to long stalks,
sopped with rain and thrown about violently,
as Paul was from his horse by the voice of Christ,
as those he judged & condemned were, leaving
        the earth;
and, deeper in, tight little buds that seem to blush
from the pleasure they take in being submissive,
because absolute humility in the face of cruelty
is the Passive's way of becoming himself;
the groan of it all, like a penetrated body –
those of us who hear it know the feeling.

SWIMMERS

Tossed
by the muscular sea,
we are lost,
and glad to be lost
in troughs of rough

love. A bath in
laughter, our dive
into foam,
our upslide and float
on the surf of desire.

But sucked to the root
of the water-mountain –
immense –
about to tip upon us
the terror of total

delight –
we are towed,
helpless in its
swell, by hooks
of our hair;

then dangled, let go,
made to race –
as the wrestling chest
of the sea, itself
tangled, tumbles

in its own embrace.
Our limbs like eels
are water-boned,
our faces lost
to difference and

contour, as the lapping
crests.
They cease
their charge,
and rock us

in repeating hammocks
of the releasing
tide –
until supine we glide,
on cool green

smiles
of an exhaling
gladiator,
to the shore
of sleep.

ANXIETY

"AFRAID OF LOSING YOU"

Afraid of losing you

I ran fluttering
like a little girl
after her mother

SAPPHO

TRANSLATED BY MARY BARNARD

LOVE'S ENTREATY

Thou knowest, love, I know that thou dost know
that I am here more near to thee to be,
and knowest that I know thou knowest me:
what means it then that we are sundered so?

If they are true, these hopes that from thee flow,
if it is real, this sweet expectancy,
break down the wall that stands 'twixt me and thee;
for pain in prison pent hath double woe.

Because in thee I love, O my loved lord,
what thou best lovest, be not therefore stern:
souls burn for souls, spirits to spirits cry!

I seek the splendour in thy fair face stored;
yet living man that beauty scarce can learn,
and he who fain would find it, first must die.

"HOURS CONTINUING LONG"

Hours continuing long, sore and heavy-hearted,
Hours of the dusk, when I withdraw to a lonesome and
    unfrequented spot, seating myself, leaning my
    face in my hands;
Hours sleepless, deep in the night, when I go forth,
    speeding swiftly the country roads, or through
    the city streets, or pacing miles and miles, stifling
    plaintive cries;
Hours discouraged, distracted – for the one I cannot
    content myself without, soon I saw him content
    himself without me;
Hours when I am forgotten, (O weeks and months are
    passing, but I believe I am never to forget!)
Sullen and suffering hours! (I am ashamed – but it is
    useless – I am what I am;)
Hours of my torment – I wonder if other men ever
    have the like, out of the like feelings?
Is there even one other like me – distracted – his friend,
    his lover, lost to him?
Is he too as I am now? Does he still rise in the
    morning, dejected, thinking who is lost to him?
    and at night, awaking, think who is lost?
Does he too harbour his friendship silent and endless?
    harbour his anguish and passion?

Does some stray reminder, or casual mention of a
    name, bring the fit back upon him, taciturn and
    deprest?
Doe he see himself reflected in me? In these hours,
    does he see the face of his hours reflected?

THE TAXI

When I go away from you
The world beats dead
Like a slackened drum.
I call out for you against the jutted stars
And shout into the ridges of the wind.
Streets coming fast,
One after the other,
Wedge you away from me,
And the lamps of the city prick my eyes
So that I can no longer see your face.
Why should I leave you,
To wound myself upon the sharp edges of the night?

AMY LOWELL

TO EROS

In that I loved you, Love, I worshipped you.
In that I worshipped well, I sacrificed.
All of most worth I bound and burnt and slew:
Old peaceful lives; frail flowers; firm friends;
     and Christ.

I slew all falser loves; I slew all true,
That I might nothing love but your truth, Boy.
Fair fame I cast away as bridegrooms do
Their wedding garments in their haste of joy.

But when I fell upon your sandalled feet,
You laughed; you loosed away my lips; you rose.
I heard the singing of your wings' retreat;
Far-flown, I watched you flush the Olympian snows,
Beyond my hoping. Starkly I returned
To stare upon the ash of all I burned.

"DEAR TO ME NOW"

Dear to me now and longer than a summer,
Not like an ugly cousin starved for love
Or prisoned in the tower of a stammer,
Through sharpened senses peer into my life
With insight and loathing; but sigh and sign
Interpret simply like an animal
That finds the fenced-in pasture very green,
No hint of malice in the trainer's call.

Elsewhere these hands have hurt, these lips betrayed,
This will has quarrelled under different names,
The proofs of love have had to be destroyed
Or lost their whole assurance many times.
See in my eyes the look you look to see;
I may be false but O be true to me.

THE PEDLAR

Lend me, a little while, the key
    That locks your heavy heart, and I'll give you back –
Rarer than books and ribbons and beads bright to see,
    This little Key of Dreams out of my pack.

The road, the road, beyond men's bolted doors,
    There shall I walk and you go free of me,
For yours lies North across the moors,
    And mine South. To what sea?

How if we stopped and let our solemn selves go by,
    While my gay ghost caught and kissed yours, as
        ghosts don't do,
And by the wayside this forgotten you and I
    Sat, and were twenty-two?

Give me the key that locks your tired eyes,
    And I will lend you this one from my pack,
Brighter than coloured beads and painted books that
        make men wise:
    Take it. No, give it back!

ADVICE TO YOUTH
(For Guillaume)

Since little time is granted here
　　For pride in pain or play,
Since blood soon cools before that Fear
　　That makes our prowess clay,
If lips to kiss are freely met,
　　Lad, be not proud nor shy;
There are no lips where men forget,
　　And undesiring lie.

COUNTEE CULLEN　　　　　　　　　187

YOU AND I

Who are you?
A surface warm to my fingers,
a solid form, an occupant of space,
a makeshift kind of enjoyment,
a pitiless being who runs away like water,
something left unfinished, out of inferior matter,

Something God thought of.
Nothing, sometimes everything,
something I cannot believe in,
a foolish argument, you, yourself, not I,
an enemy of mine. My lover.

Who am I?
A wounded man, badly bandaged,
a monster among angels or angel among monsters,
a box of questions shaken up and scattered on the floor,

A foot on the stairs, a voice on a wire,
a busy collection of thumbs that imitate fingers,
an enemy of yours. Your lover.

THE RING

Love is the master of the ring
And life a circus tent.
What is this silly song you sing?
Love is the master of the ring.

I am afraid!
Afraid of Love
And of Love's bitter whip!
Afraid,
Afraid of Love
And Love's sharp, stinging whip.

What is this silly song you sing?
Love is the master of the ring.

RULES OF SLEEP

In the sludge drawer of animals in arms,
Where the legs entwine to keep the body warm
Against the winter night, some cold seeps through –
It is the future: say, a square of stars
In the windowpane, suggesting the abstract
And large, or a sudden shift in position
That lets one body know the other's free to move
An inch away, and then a thousand miles,
And, after that, even intimacy
Is only another form of separation.

SONG IN AUTUMN

The wind comes down before the creeping night
And you, my love, are hid within the green
Long grasses; and the dusk steals up between
Each leaf, as through the shadow quick with fright
The startled hare leaps up and out of sight.

The hedges whisper in their loaded boughs
Where warm birds slumber, pressing wing to wing,
All pulsing faintly, like a muted string
Above us where we weary of our vows —
And hidden underground the soft moles drowse.

NOCTURNE

There's nothing worse
than feeling bad and not
being able to tell you.
Not because you'd kill me
or it would kill you, or
we don't love each other.
It's space. The sky is grey
and clear, with pink and
blue shadows under each cloud.
A tiny airliner drops its
specks over the UN Building.
My eyes, like millions of
glassy squares, merely reflect.
Everything sees through me,
in the daytime I'm too hot
and at night I freeze; I'm
built the wrong way for the
river and a mild gale would
break every fiber in me.
Why don't I go east and west
instead of north and south?
It's the architect's fault.
And in a few years I'll be
useless, not even an office
building. Because you have

no telephone, and live so
far away; the Pepsi-Cola sign,
the seagulls and the noise.

BETWEEN US

A ... face? There
It lies on the pillow by
Your turned head's tangled graying hair:
Another – like a shrunken head, too small!
My eyes in dread
Shut. Open. It is there,

Waxen, inhuman. Small.
The taut crease of the mouth shifts. It
Seems to smile,
Chin up in the wan light. Elsewhere
I have known what it was, this thing, known
The blind eye-slit

And knuckle-sharp cheekbone –
Ah. And again do.
Not a face. A hand, seen queerly. Mine.
Deliver me, I breathe
Watching it unclench with a soft moan
And reach for you.

SUITE

Afterwards (July 15, 1964)

Debts writing me letters,
Mice running under my bed,
My mother's horse looks in the door,
Her fingers waltz the window pane.

O that piano in the Alps.
Louder it swells, again, again!
I wake. The moon is shining in.
Its stains are on the floor, a chair.
The smashed white clock she cannot mend again.

Nota Bene

I'll break your heart, A. said to me
You'll break my heart, I said to B.
Both did, and still, is my ticker all that smashed?
We get over old wounds by acquiring new ones,
Said C. And thus I obtained all three.

Your Words

Your words cross back from days
I try to think just when it was
You said that beautiful thing
Or chiseled that flamboyant phrase

And thinking am half lost
In pursuit again
Of how it was you looked
When your painted speeches shook
My reluctant heart.

The Beginning

You
Came drifting up to me
As a cat will seek a new home
When a summer master's left.
And I was charmed by that,
I did not ponder riddles, I esteemed
The surfaced play, the light
Inconsequential thing
And wished to be a matchfire for a moth.

And the Platonic Order

And the Platonic order of the morning, chaste,
Spontaneous, with a hot cool sun
The satin cups of the crocus, the hyacinth
Not Greek, not "ensanguined with woe,"
Already the loose knot of violets
Lead me. And I cannot go.

"THE MIND IS HUNG WITH COBWEBS"

The mind is hung with cobwebs
In a landscape of astonished ash;
Love's hurricane has passed overhead:
Not a bird left.

Nor a leaf.
They disappear like drops of water
When an ocean goes dry.
When tears are not enough
Because as cruel as a spring day of sun someone
Splits a body in two with his mere presence.

Now we need to gather up the pieces of prudence,
Though one of them is always missing,
To collect this empty life
And go along hoping it will slowly fill up
If possible, again, as before
With unrecognized dreams and invisible desires.

Oh you know nothing of this,
You are over there, as cruel as the day,
The day, the light that tightly holds some sorrowful
     wall.
A wall – can't you understand?
A wall I face alone.

LUIS CERNUDA   197
TRANSLATED BY REGINALD GIBBONS

PART OF A LETTER TO THE
CODIGNOLA BOY

Caro ragazzo, yes, sure, let's meet,
but don't expect much from this meeting.
At the least, a new disappointment, a new
emptiness: one of those meetings good
for narcissistic dignity, like a sorrow.
At forty, I'm just as I was at seventeen.
However frustrated, the middle-aged man and the kid
are able, certainly, to *meet*, hemming and hawing
over ideas held in common, over problems
that can make two decades loom, a whole lifetime,
even though they are apparently the same.
Until one word, finding its way out of uncertain
        throats,
worn out from weeping and the wish to be alone –
reveals the incurable disparity of it all.
And, with you, I will have to play the poet-
father, and then fall back on irony –
which will embarrass you: the forty-year-old
by now the master of his own life,
livelier, younger than the seventeen-year-old.
Other than this likelihood, this pretense,
I have nothing else to tell you.
I'm stingy, the little I possess
I hold tight to my diabolical heart.

And the two lengths of skin between cheekbone
        and chin,
under the mouth disfigured by forced, timid
smiles, and the eye which has lost
its sweetness, like a fig gone sour –
there might appear before you the exact
portrait of that maturity you're pained by,
a maturity not at all brotherly. Of what use to you
is a contemporary – merely withering away
in the very leanness that devours his flesh?
What he has given he's given, the rest
is exhausted compassion.

PIER PAOLO PASOLINI   199
TRANSLATED BY DAVID STIVENDER AND
J. D. McCLATCHY

A RENEWAL

Having used every subterfuge
To shake you, lies, fatigue, or even that of passion,
Now I see no way but a clean break.
I add that I am willing to bear the guilt.

You nod assent. Autumn turns windy, huge,
A clear vase of dry leaves vibrating on and on.
We sit, watching. When I next speak
Love buries itself in me, up to the hilt.

From THE AUTUMN SONNETS

If I can let you go as trees let go
Their leaves, so casually, one by one;
If I can come to know what they do know,
That fall is the release, the consummation,
Then fear of time and the uncertain fruit
Would not distemper the great lucid skies
This strangest autumn, mellow and acute.
If I can take the dark with open eyes
And call it seasonal, not harsh or strange
(For love itself may need a time of sleep),
And, treelike, stand unmoved before the change,
Lose what I lose to keep what I can keep,
The strong root still alive under the snow,
Love will endure – if I can let you go.

MAY SARTON   201

ONE ART

The art of losing isn't hard to master;
so many things seem filled with the intent
to be lost that their loss is no disaster.

Lose something every day. Accept the fluster
of lost door keys, the hour badly spent.
The art of losing isn't hard to master.

Then practice losing farther, losing faster:
places, and names, and where it was you meant
to travel. None of these will bring disaster.

I lost my mother's watch. And look! my last, or
next-to-last, of three loved houses went.
The art of losing isn't hard to master.

I lost two cities, lovely ones. And, vaster,
some realms I owned, two rivers, a continent.
I miss them, but it wasn't a disaster.

– Even losing you (the joking voice, a gesture
I love) I shan't have lied. It's evident
the art of losing's not too hard to master
though it may look like (*Write* it!) like disaster.

LOSING MY MIND

The sun comes up,
I think about you.
The coffee cup,
I think about you.
I want you so,
It's like I'm losing my mind.

The morning ends,
I think about you.
I talk to friends,
I think about you.
And do they know?
It's like I'm losing my mind.

All afternoon,
Doing every little chore,
The thought of you stays bright.
Sometimes I stand
In the middle of the floor,
Not going left,
Not going right.

I dim the lights
And think about you.
Spend sleepless nights

To think about you.
You said you loved me,
Or were you just being kind?
Or am I losing my mind?

From MORE POEMS

XI

The rainy Pleiads wester,
   Orion plunges prone,
The stroke of midnight ceases
   And I lie down alone.

The rainy Pleiads wester
   And seek beyond the sea
The head that I shall dream of
   That will not dream of me.

"FIVE-THIRTY, LITTLE ONE"

Five-thirty, little one, already light
outside. From Spanish Harlem, sun spills through
the seamless windows of my Gauloise blue
bedroom, where you're sleeping, with what freight
of dreams. Blue boat, blue boat, I'll navigate
and pilot, this dawn-watch. There's someone who
is dying, darling, and that's always true
though skin on skin we would obliterate
the fact, and mouth on mouth alive have come
to something like the equilibrium
of a light skiff on not-quite-tidal waves.
And aren't we, when we are on dry land
(with shaky sea legs) walking hand in hand
(often enough) reading the lines on graves?

LEAVING THE UNIVERSE

Can't go back
to his body. That wilderness.
A time he would let me
rest there, no other place to go.
A bedroom
full of star charts, planets tearing
free from orbit, a belt
of asteroids flying apart.
In that space
between us, the gravity
of my bed unable
to keep his body from floating
out the door.

TURNING FORTY IN THE 90's

We promised to grow old together, our dream
since years ago when we began
to celebrate our common tenderness
and touch. So here we are:

Dry, ashy skin, falling hair, losing breath
at the top of stairs, forgetting things.
Vials of Septra and AZT line the bedroom dresser
like a boy's toy army poised for attack –
your red, my blue, and the casualties are real.

Now the dimming in your man's eyes and mine.
Our bones ache as the muscles dissolve,
exposing the fragile gates of ribs, our last defense.
And we calculate pensions and premiums.
You are not yet forty-five, and I
not yet forty, but neither of us for long.

No Senior discounts here, so we clip coupons
like squirrels in late November, foraging
each remaining month or week, day or hour.
We hold together against the throb and jab
of yet another bone from out of nowhere poking
      through.
You grip the walker and I hobble with a cane.
Two witnesses for our bent generation.

HERE

everything extraneous has burned away
this is how burning feels in the fall
of the final year not like leaves in a blue
October but as if the skin were a paper lantern
full of trapped moths beating their fired wings
and yet I can lie on this hill just above you
a foot beside where I will lie myself
soon soon and for all the wrack and blubber
feel still how we were warriors when the
merest morning sun in the garden was a
kingdom after Room 1010 war is not all
death it turns out war is what little
thing you hold on to refugeed and far from home
oh sweetie will you please forgive me this
that every time I opened a box of anything
Glad Bags One-A-Days KINGSIZE was
the worst I'd think will you still be here
when the box is empty Rog Rog who will
play boy with me now that I bucket with tears
through it all when I'd cling beside you sobbing
you'd shrug it off with the quietest *I'm still
here* I have your watch in the top drawer
which I don't dare wear yet help me please
the boxes grocery home day after day
the junk that keeps men spotless but it doesn't

matter now how long they last or I
the day has taken you with it and all
there is now is burning dark the only green
is up by the grave and this little thing
of telling the hill I'm here oh I'm here

AFTERMATH

"I HAVE HAD NOT ONE WORD FROM HER"

I have had not one word from her

Frankly I wish I were dead.
When she left, she wept

a great deal; she said to
me, "This parting must be
endured, Sappho. I go unwillingly."

I said, "Go, and be happy
but remember (you know
well) whom you leave shackled by love

"If you forget me, think
of our gifts to Aphrodite
and all the loveliness that we shared

"all the violet tiaras,
braided rosebuds, dill and
crocus twined around your young neck

"myrrh poured on your head
and on soft mats girls with
all that they most wished for beside them

"while no voices chanted
choruses without ours,
no woodlot bloomed in spring without song ..."

SAPPHO   213

TRANSLATED BY MARY BARNARD

SONNET 87

Farewell, thou art too dear for my possessing,
And like enough thou know'st thy estimate:
The charter of thy worth gives thee releasing;
My bonds in thee are all determinate.
For how do I hold thee but by thy granting,
And for that riches where is my deserving?
The cause of this fair gift in me is wanting,
And so my patent back again is swerving.
Thyself thou gav'st, thy own worth then not knowing,
Or me, to whom thou gav'st it, else mistaking;
So thy great gift, upon misprision growing,
Comes home again, on better judgement making.
    Thus have I had thee as a dream doth flatter,
    In sleep a king, but waking no such matter.

APOLOGIA

Is it thy will that I should wax and wane,
    Barter my cloth of gold for hodden grey,
And at thy pleasure weave that web of pain
    Whose brightest threads are each a wasted day?

Is it thy will – Love that I love so well –
    That my Soul's House should be a tortured spot
Wherein, like evil paramours, must dwell
    The quenchless flame, the worm that dieth not?

Nay, if it be thy will I shall endure,
    And sell ambition at the common mart,
And let dull failure be my vestiture,
    And sorrow dig its grave within my heart.

Perchance it may be better so – at least
    I have not made my heart a heart of stone,
Nor starved my boyhood of its goodly feast,
    Nor walked where Beauty is a thing unknown.

Many a man hath done so; sought to fence
    In straitened bonds the soul that should be free,
Trodden the dusty road of common sense,
    While all the forest sang of liberty,

Not marking how the spotted hawk in flight
    Passed on wide pinion through the lofty air,
To where some steep untrodden mountain height
    Caught the last tresses of the Sun God's hair.

Or how the little flower be trod upon,
    The daisy, that white-feathered shield of gold,
Followed with wistful eyes the wandering sun
    Content if once its leaves were aureoled.

But surely it is something to have been
    The best belovèd for a little while,
To have walked hand in hand with Love, and seen
    His purple wings flit once across thy smile.

Ay! though the gorgèd asp of passion feed
    On my boy's heart, yet have I burst the bars,
Stood face to face with Beauty, known indeed
    The Love which moves the Sun and all the stars!

From LUCIEN LÉTINOIS

XXIV

Your voice, grave and low,
As soft at times
As a delicate velvet,
Sounding, when you spoke,
Of lovely water
Trembling over moss.

Your laughter sparkled,
So open and artless,
Frank, musical and free,
Like a bird in the echoing
Tree, who took flight
Trilling his song.

That laughter, that voice
Rise in my memory
Which everywhere sees you,
Now alive, now dead,
Like the ringing glory
Of holy martyrs.

The sadness you leave
Scatters with these murmurs

That urge, "Courage!"
To a heart in tumult,
Filled and fluttering
With such sad anxiety.

Storm, still your rage,
And let me speak
With my friend,
Who seems asleep,
But only rests
In an ancient wisdom....

TRANSLATED BY J. D. McCLATCHY

XXX

Shake hands, we shall never be friends, all's over;
   I only vex you the more I try.
All's wrong that ever I've done or said,
And nought to help it in this dull head:
   Shake hands, here's luck, good-bye.

But if you come to a road where danger
   Or guilt or anguish or shame's to share,
Be good to the lad that loves you true
And the soul that was born to die for you,
   And whistle and I'll be there.

From A SHROPSHIRE LAD

XVIII

Oh, when I was in love with you,
    Then I was clean and brave,
And miles around the wonder grew
    How well did I behave.

And now the fancy passes by,
    And nothing will remain,
And miles around they'll say that I
    Am quite myself again.

From ADDITIONAL POEMS

VII

He would not stay for me; and who can wonder?
　He would not stay for me to stand and gaze.
I shook his hand and tore my heart in sunder
　And went with half my life about my ways.

A. E. HOUSMAN

THE NEXT TABLE

He must be barely twenty-two years old –
yet I'm certain that almost that many years ago
I enjoyed the very same body.

It isn't erotic fever at all.
And I've been in the casino for a few minutes only,
so I haven't had time to drink a great deal.
I enjoyed that very same body.

And if I don't remember where, this one lapse of
     memory doesn't mean a thing.

There, now that he's sitting down at the next table,
I recognize every motion he makes – and under his
     clothes
I see again the limbs I loved, naked.

IN DESPAIR

He lost him completely. And he now tries to find
his lips in the lips of each new lover,
he tries in the union with each new lover
to convince himself that it's the same young man,
that it's to him he gives himself.

He lost him completely, as though he never existed.
He wanted, his lover said, to save himself
from the tainted, unhealthy form of sexual pleasure,
the tainted, shameful form of sexual pleasure.
There was still time, he said, to save himself.

He lost him completely, as though he never existed.
Through fantasy, through hallucination,
he tries to find his lips in the lips of other young men,
he longs to feel his kind of love once more.

CONSTANTINE CAVAFY
TRANSLATED BY EDMUND KEELEY AND
PHILIP SHERRARD

BEFORE TIME ALTERED THEM

They were full of sadness at their parting.
That wasn't what they themselves wanted: it was
    circumstances.
The need to earn a living forced one of them
to go far away – New York or Canada.
The love they felt wasn't, of course, what it once had
    been;
the attraction between them had gradually diminished,
the attraction had diminished a great deal.
But to be separated, that wasn't what they themselves
    wanted.
It was circumstances. Or maybe Fate
appeared as an artist and parted them now,
before their feeling died out completely, before Time
    altered them:
the one seeming to remain for the other always what
    he was,
the exquisite young man of twenty-four.

CONSTANTINE CAVAFY
TRANSLATED BY EDMUND KEELEY AND
PHILIP SHERRARD

SONNET TO MY FRIEND, WITH
AN IDENTITY DISC

If ever I had dreamed of my dead name
High in the heart of London, unsurpassed
By Time for ever, and the Fugitive, Fame,
There seeking a long sanctuary at last, –

Or if I onetime hoped to hide its shame,
– Shame of success, and sorrow of defeats, –
Under those holy cypresses, the same
That shade always the quiet place of Keats,

Now rather thank I God there is no risk
Of gravers scoring it with florid screed.
Let my inscription be this soldier's disc.
Wear it, sweet friend. Inscribe no date nor deed.
But may thy heart-beat kiss it, night and day,
Until the name grow blurred and fade away.

FUNERAL BLUES

Stop all the clocks, cut off the telephone,
Prevent the dog from barking with a juicy bone,
Silence the pianos and with muffled drum
Bring out the coffin, let the mourners come.

Let aeroplanes circle moaning overhead
Scribbling on the sky the message He Is Dead,
Put crêpe bows round the white necks of the public
        doves,
Let the traffic policemen wear black cotton gloves.

He was my North, my South, my East and West,
My working week and my Sunday rest,
My noon, my midnight, my talk, my song;
I thought that love would last for ever: I was wrong.

The stars are not wanted now: put out every one;
Pack up the moon and dismantle the sun;
Pour away the ocean and sweep up the wood;
For nothing now can ever come to any good.

SONGS FROM THE HOUSE OF DEATH, OR HOW TO MAKE IT THROUGH TO THE END OF A RELATIONSHIP
For Donald Hall

1.
From the house of death there is rain.
From rain is flood and flowers.
And flowers emerge through the ruins
of those who left behind
stores of corn and dishes,
turquoise and bruises
from the passion
of fierce love.

2.
I run my tongue over the skeleton
jutting from my jaw. I taste
the grit of heartbreak.

3.
The procession of spirits
who walk out of their bodies
is ongoing. Just as the procession
of those who have loved us
will go about their business
of making a new house
with someone else who smells
like the dust of a strange country.

4.
The weight of rain is unbearable to the sky
eventually. Just as desire will
burn a hole through the sky
and fall to earth.

5.
I was surprised by the sweet embrace
of the perfume of desert flowers after the rain
though after all these seasons
I shouldn't be surprised.

6.
All cities will be built and then destroyed.
We built too near the house of the gods of lightning,
too close to the edge of a century.
What could I expect,
my bittersweet.

7.
Even death who is the chief of everything
on this earth (all undertakings, all matters of human
form) will wash his hands, stop to rest under
the cottonwood before taking you from me
on the back of his horse.

8.
Nothing I can sing
will bring you back.
Not the songs of a hundred horses running
until they become wind.
Not the personal song of the rain
who makes love to the earth.

9.
I will never forget you. Your nakedness
haunts me in the dawn when I cannot distinguish your
flushed brown skin from the burning horizon,
      or my hands.
The smell of chaos lingers in the clothes
you left behind. I hold you
there.

THE EMBRACE

You weren't well or really ill yet either;
just a little tired, your handsomeness
tinged by grief or anticipation, which brought
to your face a thoughtful deepening grace.

I didn't for a moment doubt you were dead.
I knew that to be true still, even in the dream.
You'd been out – at work maybe? –
having a good day, almost energetic.

We seemed to be moving from some old house
where we'd lived, boxes everywhere, things
in disarray; that was the *story* of my dream,
but even asleep I was shocked out of narrative

by your face, the physical fact of your face;
inches from mine, smooth-shaven, loving, alert.
Why so difficult, remembering the actual look
of you? Without a photograph, without strain?

So when I saw your unguarded, reliable face,
your unmistakable gaze opening all the warmth
and clarity of you – warm brown tea – we held
each other for the time the dream allowed.

Bless you. You came back, so I could see you
once more, plainly, so I could rest against you
without thinking this happiness lessened anything,
without thinking you were alive again.

REQUIEM

In the sudden white silence, where are you? It seems I carry a letter to you, but the mouth of the mailbox is choked with snow and the box billows, swollen to twice its size by the thick coating of so many flakes already fallen for hours.

I think then to telephone you, seeing a booth, its panes pasted over and opaque like a half-marbled sentry box. But the floor is so deep in snow that I cannot pull the door to. Even the books are thick in it and the mouthpiece is sifted over.

Balked, I walk into the park of the trees of this new foliage, false orchard bewildering like a fruitless spring. From afar strikes one bell practising to be heard.

Is it you calling?

No. Only my heart tolling.

AMOR VINCIT OMNIA

Love is no more.
It died as the mind dies: the pure desire
Relinquishing the blissful form it wore,
The ample joy and clarity expire.

Regret is vain.
Then do not grieve for what you would efface,
The sudden failure of the past, the pain
Of its unwilling change, and the disgrace.

Leave innocence,
And modify your nature by the grief
Which poses to the will indifference
That no desire is permanent in sense.

Take leave of me.
What recompense, or pity, or deceit
Can cure, or what assumed serenity
Conceal the mortal loss which we repeat?

The mind will change, and change shall be relief.

LOVE-LETTER-BURNING

The archivist in us shudders at such cold-
blooded destruction of the word, but since
we're only human, we commit our sins
to the flames. Sauve qui peut; fear makes us bold.

Tanka was bolder: when the weather turned
from fair to frigid, he saw his way clear
to build a sacrificial fire
in which a priceless temple Buddha burned.

(The pretext? Simple: what he sought
was legendary Essence in the ash.
But if it shows up only in the flesh – ?
He grinned and said, Let's burn the lot!)

Believers in the afterlife perform
this purifying rite. At last
a match is struck: it's done. The past
will shed some light, but never keep us warm.

BLUES/FOR J.C.

Letting go, woman, is not as easy as pride
or commitment
to civilization would
have us think. Loveletters crowding against the will:

The esplanade of your belly, I said, *that*
shallow and gleaming spoon. You
said, *Not quite*
an epiphany, our bodies breathing
like greedy gills, *not quite*
an epiphany, but close, close. I loved you

then for that
willful precision, the same
precision with which you now
extricate
cool as a surgeon
your amphibian heart. My mouth,

blind in the night to pride, circles
your absence, absurd as one
fish, kissing
compulsively through the vertigo
of the deep

silence
an ocean, dimly perceived
like an aftertaste: my own salt, my fish-
bowl gyrations, my beached
up mouth.

LATE NIGHT ODE
Horace IV.i

It's over, love. Look at me pushing fifty now,
    Hair like grave-grass growing in both ears,
The piles and boggy prostate, the crooked penis,
    The sour taste of each day's first lie,

And that recurrent dream of years ago pulling
    A swaying bead-chain of moonlight,
Of slipping between the cool sheets of dark
    Along a body like my own, but blameless.

What good's my cut-glass conversation now,
    Now I'm so effortlessly vulgar and sad?
You get from life what you can shake from it?
    For me, it's g and t's all day and CNN.

Try the blond boychick lawyer, entry level
    At eighty grand, who pouts about the overtime,
Keeps Evian and a beeper in his locker at the gym,
    And hash in tinfoil under the office fern.

There's your hound from heaven, with buccaneer
    Curls and perfumed war-paint on his nipples.
His answering machine always has room for one more
    Slurred, embarrassed call from you-know-who.

237

Some nights I've laughed so hard the tears
   Won't stop. Look at me now. Why *now*?
I long ago gave up pretending to believe
   Anyone's memory will give as good as it gets.

So why these stubborn tears? And why do I dream
   Almost every night of holding you again,
Or at least of diving after you, my long-gone,
   Through the bruised unbalanced waves?

ANNIVERSARY

He too must with me wash his body, though
at far distant time, over endless space
take the cloth unto his loins, upon his face
engage in the self same *toilette* as I do now.

Cigarette between his lips, would they were mine
by this present moon swear allegiance
if he ever look, see clouds and breaches
in the sky, by stars lend his eyes shine.

What care I for miles, rows of friends lined
up in groups, blue songs, day's bright glare.
Once he was there, now gone searched empty air
this candle feeds on, find eyes, my heart's blind

to love and all he was capable of, sweet patience
when he put his lips to places I cannot name
because changed, now not the same
sun shines sad larks break forth
from winter branches.

THEN

When I am dead, even then,
I will still love you, I will wait in these poems,
When I am dead, even then
I am still listening to you.
I will still be making poems for you
out of silence;
silence will be falling into that silence,
it is building music.

ACKNOWLEDGMENTS

Thanks are due to the following copyright holders for their permission to reprint:

ACKLAND, VALENTINE: 'When I have said' by Valentine Ackland from *The Nature of the Moment* by Valentine Ackland and Sylvia Townsend Warner, published by Chatto & Windus. Used by permission of the Executors of the Sylvia Townsend Warner Estate and The Random House Group Limited. 'The eyes of the body, being blindfold by night' by Valentine Ackland from *Whether a Dove or a Seagull* by Valentine Ackland and Sylvia Townsend Warner, published by Chatto & Windus. Used by permission of the Executors of the Sylvia Townsend Warner Estate and The Random House Group Limited. AUDEN, W. H.: 'A Lullaby', 'Funeral Blues', copyright 1940 and renewed 1968 by W. H. Auden, 'Fish in the unruffled lakes', copyright 1937 and renewed 1965 by W. H. Auden, 'What's in your mind, my dove', copyright 1934 and renewed 1962 by W. H. Auden, from *W. H. Auden: Collected Poems* by W. H. Auden, copyright © 1976 by Edward Mendelson, William Meredith and Monroe K. Spears, Executors of the Estate of W. H. Auden. Used by permission of Random House, Inc. in the U.S. and by the publishers, Faber and Faber Ltd. in the U.K. 'Dear to me now and longer than a summer' from *The English Auden* by W. H. Auden, reprinted by permission of the publishers, Faber and Faber Ltd. BALDWIN, JAMES: 'Munich, Winter 1973' © 1983 by James Baldwin. Collected in *Jimmy's Blues*, published by St. Martin's Press. Reprinted by arrangement with the James Baldwin

247

INDEX OF AUTHORS